Goethe and Inner Harmony

Goethe
and Inner Harmony

A study of the 'schöne Seele' in the
Apprenticeship of Wilhelm Meister

Daniel J. Farrelly

BOOKS
10 East 53d St., New York 10022
(a division of Harper & Row Publishers, Inc.)

Published in the U.S.A. 1973 by:
Harper & Row Publishers, Inc.
Barnes & Noble Import Division

ISBN 06-492067-4

All forms of micropublishing   .
© *Irish University Microforms   Shannon   Ireland*

Printed in the Republic of Ireland

For my Mother

Contents

My thanks are due to Professor Gusdorf, of Strasbourg University, for the interest he showed in this study, as also to his colleagues, Professor Canivez and Professor Fink, for their advice and constructive criticism. Professor Diethelm Brüggemann and Professor John O'Meara of University College, Dublin, showed their interest in energetic, practical terms which helped speed the book on its way to the printers. Jutta Rosen assisted with reliable, accurate work in the final preparation of the manuscript.

My thanks are due also to University College, Dublin, for a generous grant which helped advance the date of publication.

My special thanks are due to several of my friends—and particularly to my wife—who shared the longueurs paradoxically involved in writing a relatively short book.

D.F.

I

Introduction

When Goethe first attempted to write a novel on Wilhelm Meister—
calling it *Wilhelm Meister's Vocation to the Theatre*—he managed to
complete only six books. Then he found he was unable to proceed with
the work. When he later took up the fragment with the intention of re-
working it, he had advanced well into his classical period. This transition was deeply significant both for the style of life he led and for his
approach to creative literature. The new version of the novel, now
called *Wilhelm Meister's Apprenticeship*, supremely classical though it
was, still bore traces of its origins: critics[1] have been acutely aware of
the exuberance and liveliness of the early books of the *Apprenticeship*
and have contrasted them with the controlled, mature and even cool
tone of the seventh and eighth (the two final) books of the novel, which
are entirely the product of his classical period.[2]

In between these two different blocks, one still betraying the influence
of the young Goethe and the other typical of the classical Goethe, a
section is inserted which presents a puzzle for the critics. This is the
sixth book, entitled *Bekenntnisse einer schönen Seele*—*Confessions of a
beautiful soul* would be the literal translation; here we shall refer to this
section of the novel simply as the *Confession*. This section constitutes
Goethe's attempt to work the transition between the two different phases
both of his creative life and of his creative work. Wilhelm, the confused
and undisciplined apprentice whose liberation from the bourgeois at-
mosphere of his home led to his vagabond, unconventional existence
amongst a troup of actors, was eventually to be introduced into the
serene, ordered, classically enlightened world symbolized by the heroine

---

1   See, for example, Pascal, *The German Novel*, p. 27.
2   The first four books of the *Lehrjahre* together with a part of the fifth
    book constitute the revised version of the orignal six books of *Wilhelm
    Meisters Theatralische Sendung*.

1

Natalie. This transition was prepared for in various ways, the most striking of these being Wilhelm's contact with the *Confession*.

Wilhelm's friend Aurelie, an actress, became seriously ill. When she was faced with death, a doctor lent her a manuscript with the intention of helping her to a calmer frame of mind. Wilhelm himself read the manuscript and was deeply impressed by it. He later found out that this *Confession* was written by Natalie's aunt. This manuscript interrupts the action of the novel, forming a sharp contrast to Wilhelm's confused and agitated experience. It gives the impression, according to Schiller, that the story comes to a standstill.[3] After the bustle and movement of the first five books it sets a quiet, meditative tone which forms a prelude to the classical harmony and serenity of the world Wilhelm is to enter.

Strangely enough, the tone of this sixth book is, according to the critics, so different from that of the two parts it unites that there is serious doubt as to whether Goethe wrote it himself or merely incorporated into his novel a manuscript written by Susanna Katherina von Klettenberg, a relative of his mother and a friend of the young writer. Testimony given by Goethe's mother seems to conflict with what Goethe himself said.[4] In any event, Charlotte von Stein's bitter judgment that Goethe was prepared to include another's manuscript in his novel so long as the publishers paid for it was hardly a balanced appraisal. The critics now seem satisfied that the basis for the *Confession* was a series of Susanna's letters and conversations which Goethe drew on and shaped for his own purposes.[5] It has not been decided how extensively Goethe borrowed from this source. In any case, Goethe felt that he had achieved his aim in writing the sixth book. Despite a certain feeling of estrangement with regard to the book and its subject matter, he wrote joyfully to Schiller that: 'I have managed to pilot the ship past the rocks.'[6]

But more important than deciding how much of the *Confession* is to be attributed to Goethe himself is the task of appreciating, on the one hand, the integral role that the *Confession* plays in the novel as a whole and, on the other hand, the artistic value of the novel itself. The doubts about the authorship of the *Confession* have made it much easier to discredit the experience with which it deals: if it is not authentically Goethean it can be explained away as an oddity, a curiosity to be looked at briefly and passed over. But such doubts do not excuse the critic from subjecting the *Confession* itself to close scrutiny in an attempt to fathom

---

3   See Schiller's letter to Goethe, 17 August 1795.

4   See Riemann, *Goethes Romantechnik*, p. 17.

5   'Briefe und Unterhaltungen'—see Goethe, *Dichtung und Wahrheit*, edited by Erich Trunz, vol. 9, p. 338.

6   18 August 1795.

its meaning—page by page. The critic's aim should be to show the relevance which the experience contained in the *Confession* has to the novel as a whole. Goethe himself said of the sixth book that it 'points forwards and backwards and, by setting limits, it at the same time leads and guides.'[7] Our task in this study is to arrive at a more fundamental grasp of the experience concretized in the *Confession*.

It is clear that the fate of the heroine, Natalie, is inseparably linked with that of her aunt, the 'schöne Seele' of the *Confession*. The links between them are so obvious (see chapter 5, below) that rejection of the aunt necessarily entails undervaluing Natalie. If our study throws light on the aunt's experience, it is to be expected that in the long run our understanding of Natalie will be enriched—though we will content ourselves here with pointing up the broad lines of this interaction.

The most striking link between Natalie and her aunt is provided in the title of the *Confession*. The aunt is called: 'schöne Seele'. We don't know her in the novel by any other name. The other references to her are as 'aunt' (Tante), and as Phyllis, which is obviously a classical allusion rather than her own name.[8] The appellation 'schöne Seele' is eventually given to Natalie herself who, according to her brother Lothario, is even more deserving of the title than their aunt.[9]

It is not possible to give here an adequate account of what Goethe meant by 'schöne Seele'. For both Goethe and Schiller the expression referred, in general terms, to a harmonious quality in persons who belonged in their world and were also at one with themselves. Again in general terms, for Goethe this meant a harmonious integration of the person with nature as found in the person himself and in the world around him, whereas for Schiller the emphasis was different: the harmony which was more typical of him was the marriage between duty and inclination: the spontaneous doing of what one should.

But with this formal distinction between Goethe's and Schiller's conception of the 'schöne Seele' the final word has not been said. Only after a great deal of research will it be possible to give an adequately differentiated account of what is to be understood by Goethe's 'schöne Seele'. Undoubtedly Natalie is the finest, most perfect example of this phenomenon, and any definitive study of Goethe's conception of the 'schöne Seele' would have to be centred on her. But before beginning with Natalie herself, important foundations can and should be laid by devoting a careful study to the person from whom she steals the title, a

---

7   18 March 1795.

8   *Lehrjahre*, p. 363, 36. The edition of the novel referred to throughout will be the German Hamburger Ausgabe of *Goethes Werke*, vol. VII, edited by Erich Trunz (1962). The English translations follow Carlyle as far as possible.

9   *Lehrjahre*, p. 608, 19ff.

person whom she supersedes without destroying the organic continuity between herself and the other. This person is no other than the one who, in the *Confession*, describes her inner experience in considerable detail.

A brief glance at the history of the notion of 'schöne Seele' could help as an introduction to our task. Hans Schmeer traces the concept back as far as Plato, who has the idea of 'schöne Seele' though he never uses the expression *psychè kalé*.[10] The notion is more important for Plotinus, who often speaks about the psyche's beauty though without using the expression 'schöne Seele'.[11] He goes no further than saying *he psyché kalé:* the soul is beautiful.[12] It is important for our purposes to note that he also identifies the beautiful with the good: thus the 'schöne Seele' is necessarily dependent on the ethical sphere, which in the *Confession* plays an important though, as we shall see, not a primary role.

The 'pulchritudo animi' found in Latin literature is not common to the whole of Roman culture, but stems from stoic circles.[13] Here, in a way that anticipates the 'schöne Seele' of the *Confession*, the accent is laid on evenness, harmony and a certain firmness and constancy, which we will see are clearly characteristic of the aunt's inner attitude.

A further step which also throws light on the *Confession* is the linking of the notion with Christian mysticism. The central aspect of the soul's beauty is no longer the ethical human striving and constancy but the way the soul is affected by grace.[14] This religious basis for the inner beauty is of extreme importance in the experience of the aunt. The relationship of the ethical and the religious in the *Confession* will become apparent in the course of our study. Because of the religious dimension, this particular 'schöne Seele' shows a profound affinity not only with St Augustine's mysticism but also with that of the medieval period, where the religious basis continued to be the primary aspect of beauty of soul, innocence and humility being its essential characteristics.[15] The bridal mysticism based on the *Canticle of Canticles* is another link between the Middle Ages and the *Confession*.[16] Nobility of soul is constituted not by birth but by the capacity for love. The soul in love with the divine spouse becomes beautiful through the encounter with him. In the *Confession* this bridal imagery is found, and it becomes clear that the aunt's inner harmony (which makes her 'beautiful') depends

---

10   Hans Schmeer, 'Der Begriff der "schönen Seele"'. *Germanische Studien,* vol. 44, p. 1.

11   Ibid.

12   Ibid.

13   Ibid., p. 2.

14   Ibid.

15   Ibid., p. 3.

16   Ibid.

directly on the primacy given in her experience to the divine element. The development of the notion 'schöne Seele' proceeds further with the transition into the modern world. The Spanish mystics of the sixteenth century are responsible for the inclusion of a new element in the notion. The new role played by feeling in the life of the mystics forms the basis for the sentimentality which was prevalent in England, France and Germany in the eighteenth century.[17] Attention was focussed on the mystic's inner personal response. Thus, as Schmeer points out: 'St Thérèse is the typical highly-strung, refined, psychic individual; she is the typical *schöne Seele*.'[18] This influence was very marked in the French mystics of the seventeenth century, such as Francis de Sales and Mme Guyon. The development culminated in Fénelon's defence of Mme Guyon against the unsentimental attacks of the more traditional Bossuet. Suspected of quietism, Fénelon was condemned and he renounced the suspect elements of his mystical theology.[19] But his capitulation did nothing to diminish his influence, which spread to other countries through the mystics Poiret, Jurieu and Elias Saurin.[20]

But another aspect of the 'schöne Seele' appeared in Germany where beauty was seen as the manifestation of moral perfection. Beauty became an attribute of virtue.[21] Greater religious depth was given to the notion by the pietist movement which, in its attitude towards beauty, was much more in line with the mysticism of Augustine and the medieval mystics than with Baroque Germany. Evidence of this is seen, for example, in the bridal mysticism which we have already referred to in connection with the medieval mystics and which was important for the pietists. It also provides a link between pietism and the Spanish mystics.

The development of the concept 'schöne Seele' in modern times comes from at least two relatively independent streams: the Spanish-French sentimental stream and the German pietist stream (the German Baroque contribution being largely an impoverishment rather than an enrichment or development of the notion).[22] With regard to the 'schöne Seele' of the *Confession*, the question arises about the affinity of this particular 'schöne Seele' to the two different streams. Is the aunt's 'parentage' as a 'schöne Seele' to be sought in the sentimental line or is it more basically a product of pietism?

Here a preliminary distinction needs to be drawn. We can agree with Schmeer that the expression 'schöne Seele' as a title of the *Confession*

---

17 Ibid., p. 4.
18 Ibid.
19 Wieser, *Der sentimentale Mensch*, p. 75.
20 Ibid.
21 Schmeer, 'Der Begriff der "schönen Seele",' p. 5.
22 Ibid.

comes from the sentimental tradition.[23] But the phenomenon of the particular 'schöne Seele', the individual person who makes the *Confession*, is in our opinion much closer to the pietist than to the sentimental stream.

Firstly, with regard to the expression 'schöne Seele': as Schmeer says,[24] Goethe was less concerned with clarifying the concept than with creating an individual instance representing the type, 'schöne Seele'. For this reason, the words of the expression 'schöne Seele' are not as important for Goethe as the qualities that combine to constitute the type. Thus it is no surprise that we find, as Schmeer points out,[25] that in *Tasso*, the *Unterhaltungen deutscher Ausgewanderten*, *Wahlverwandtschaften*, *Wilhelm Meisters Theatralische Sendung*, and the *Wanderjahre* the expression does not occur even once. In *Iphigenie*, where the heroine must be considered as one of the purest manifestations of the 'schöne Seele' in Goethe, the expression is used only twice, once with reference to Orest (2, 2) and once with reference to Iphigenie herself (4, 2).

Schmeer discusses how Goethe came to use the term in the title of the *Confession*. He expresses the opinion that Goethe was influenced by his exposure to the general stream of sentimentality rather than, say, to something as specific as pietism. Although there are very definite traces of pietism in the *Confession*, there is no conclusive evidence that Goethe derives the title of his book from the pietist movement. In the first place, the expression is not a typically pietist one; secondly, it is not an expression used in the letters of Goethe's pietist friend Susanna Katherina von Klettenberg, on whose life the *Confession* is at least modelled (if it is too much to say that she was substantially its author).[26]

It seems safe to agree with Schmeer that Goethe himself was not primarily interested in the concept of 'schöne Seele'. He had a particular concrete manifestation of human life in mind, something that he believed was worth portraying. Whether or not it measured up to a concept like 'schöne Seele' was another question which would have been of far greater interest to a theoretician and philosopher like Schiller than to Goethe.

What interests us above all in this study is not to what extent Goethe's 'schöne Seele' (in the *Confession*) measures up to any given definition of the notion, but to take this manifestation of human experience and analyse it. Close inspection should show that a great deal of criticism of Natalie's aunt, both in Goethe's time and in our own, is based on a considerable misunderstanding of her experience. It is our aim here to

23 Ibid., p. 64.
24 Ibid., p. 62.
25 Ibid.
26 Ibid., p. 63.

examine the structure of this experience and see whether it is basically a genuine and healthy attitude towards life (with some clear limitations) or whether it is merely a manifestation of the sentimentality of the eighteenth century which could not survive except as a literary curiosity, a psychological aberration.

2
Relationship to Sentimentalism

Contrasting the aunt's type of experience with that of eighteenth-century sentimentalism should serve as a useful basis for clearing away misunderstandings about Natalie's aunt and thus leave us more free to appreciate her positive qualities. Without giving any detailed historical account of the sentimentalism of the period (which, as Max Wieser's book shows,[1] is a complex task well beyond the scope of our study) we can discuss some of the main characteristics of the sentimental person and relate them to the aunt's inner attitudes. Then in the course of our scrutiny of the *Confession* we will be able to see in more detail that the aunt's experience is more genuinely religious than that of the sentimental person. To reject her as egocentric and preoccupied with her own feelings would be justifiable, if one could produce the necessary evidence; if, on the other hand, her experience is seen as totally different, not egocentric but preoccupied with a reality which she is convinced stands over against her and is not merely reducible to being a creation of her own subjectivity, then our rejection or acceptance of her experience will reflect our own convictions about this kind of experience. If we are convinced, *a priori* to reading the novel, that religious experience can only reflect some kind of aberration and cannot correspond to anything real, then the aunt can hardly hope for appreciation from us; if, on the other hand, we are open to this possibility and are willing to see what the aunt's experience means for her, then we have a chance of doing her justice. A further attitude on the part of the reader is possible: to be convinced that such religious experience is vital for a profound understanding of human existence. In this case, the aunt's chances of being appreciated are at their best. But the openness of the *second* attitude is all that is required.

---

1   Wieser, *Der sentimentale Mensch.*

9

Natalie's own criticism of her aunt can serve as an introduction to this section:

> Very weak health, perhaps too much preoccupation with herself combined with a moral and religious scrupulosity prevented her from being to the world what in other circumstances she might have been. (8, 3).

> Eine sehr schwache Gesundheit, vielleicht zu viel Beschäftigung mit sich selbst, und dabei eine sittliche und religöse Ängstlichkeit liessen sie das der Welt nicht sein, was sie unter anderen Umständen hätte werden können.[2]

Natalie, in Max Wieser's terminology, is the 'naïve' person who resembles a plant growing in complete harmony with its environment,[3] completely unified in itself and living healthily with its roots deep down in the life-giving soil. Natalie is secure, natural, she belongs in her world. Contrasting with this 'naïve' kind of person there are two other types, which Wieser carefully distinguishes as the 'sentimentalisch' and the 'sentimental' person.[4] Both of these have in common that they do not fit spontaneously, effortlessly into their environment. They tend to be isolated from the world around them and are aware of sharp contrasts between themselves and others. A tension is set up between their own ideals and the world in which they would have to accomplish their ideals.

What distinguishes the 'sentimentalisch' from the 'sentimental' person is the difference in the way each reacts to this tension. A person is 'sentimentalisch' if he consciously withstands the tension and suffers from the isolation imposed on him. Basically he strives to work a synthesis between his own inner life and the world around him, but if the task is impossible he suffers his isolation as something unavoidably inflicted on him. If he does not fit into the world around him, it is because basic conflicts belong to real existence and he, caught up in the real problems of life, is exposed to such conflicts. The person who is 'sentimental', on the other hand, is one who cannot stand the conflict and withdraws into himself. His isolation is self-imposed as a flight from outside pressures. The person who is 'sentimentalisch' fights a losing (or victorious) battle in his attempt to achieve the synthesis between the inner and outer world; the person who is 'sentimental' avoids suffering defeat and retires to ground where there can be no battle.

Our contention here is to show that the 'schöne Seele' of the *Confes-*

---

2   *Lehrjahre*, p. 517, 34ff.
3   *Der sentimentale Mensch*, p. 3.
4   Ibid.

sion was forced into isolation from the world, and genuinely suffered from the contrast between her own ideals and the world around her. She did not simply retire within herself to a point where there was no battle. She was defeated but did not resign herself inwardly to the defeat. The sentimental person would have given up even inner resistance and wallowed in the feeling of defeat.

In the case of the sentimental person, feeling becomes divorced from reality and is enjoyed for its own sake. If a person sacrifices his career, the feelings accompanying the sacrifice could be bitter sorrow at the loss of something very dear, like the opportunity to develop and exploit a talent that he values highly and that has in the past given his life a great deal of meaning. The person who is 'sentimentalisch' will experience the pain of such a basic sacrifice, even while recognizing the need for his course of action. The conflict between his ideals and the world around him may impose this sacrifice on him, and a strongly principled person may find the strength to make the sacrifice. The 'sentimental' person is different. To him, the sacrifice would have a different meaning: his reason for making it might be that he feels inadequate to carry out the normal demands of a difficult vocation and he opts out of it before it becomes apparent (he fears) that he is not fully equipped for the task. His retreat is all the more palatable to him if it can be made to look like a genuine sacrifice demanded of him by some high principle. Once he has made his 'sacrifice' he will cherish the notion that he is a victim and will enjoy the feeling of victimization. In reality he is not a victim at all; his sacrifice is self-imposed because he finds it more pleasant to organize his own failure than to have one imposed on him by forces beyond his control. He can retire and enjoy the feeling of victimization. The sacrifice is not real and for this reason his feeling of being a victim is unreal. Sentimentality involves feeling which has no relationship to anything real. By contrast, the person who is 'sentimentalisch' will have the sacrifice imposed on him because of his courageous stance on a principle to which he knows himself committed; the sacrifice itself is real, and the feeling is one of pain or sorrow because he values what he has lost; if the feeling lasts, this will be because the awareness of and attachment to the thing sacrificed remain, and not because of any enjoyment of one's own plight as a sufferer.

When the aunt herself suffers, her reflections on and analyses of her states of mind do not betray evidence of sentimentality. Keen psychological awareness of one's own states of mind is not identical with any morbid preoccupation with oneself, and it seems to me that even Natalie's gentle criticism of her aunt is not borne out by what we are shown of her in the *Confession*. When she loses Narziss, for example, this results from a clear decision on her part after a good deal of experience of his qualities and thought about the possibility of a relationship with him: there is no suggestion of a wallowing in feelings of loneliness. Her decisiveness and determination betray none of the hankerings and yearnings for the past and for what she has lost. In this important episode of her life she shows herself unsentimental in a high degree.

Natalie's reference to her moral and religious scrupulosity would seem to indicate that the aunt has at least some of the sentimental person's characteristics. Max Wieser refers to the tendency in the sentimental person to speak a lot about morality, to moralize, without actually showing moral strength.[5] Along with his preoccupation with moral questions, the sentimentalist—as Wieser describes him—is a person who compromises readily; his subtlety of thought and ability to appreciate the most divergent points of view make it difficult for him to arrive at a practical decision; thus, despite a show of action, he is seldom the active, decisive type. His lack of action and his retirement from the world around him are both rooted in indecisiveness and inner insecurity. Though the aunt herself lived in comparative retirement and was hardly an active type, the explanation for this lay not with any indecision on her part. A close scrutiny of the text makes it abundantly clear that she was capable of making definite decisions and acting on them in a consistent, realistic way. (If she is to be criticized, a better foundation could be found in her toughness towards Narziss and her relatives.) As we shall see, her strength, courage and definiteness in making decisions grew with the growing depth of her religious experience; this inner attitude does not square with that of the vacillating sentimental person who cannot make a decision for fear of hurting those whom his decision will affect. (The aunt's courage in this respect does not, in my opinion, reflect any kind of insensitivity. Choice demands some kind of rejection, and courage to choose includes both courage to say 'yes' to the person or object chosen and courage to say 'no' to the person or object not chosen; the person who chooses needs the courage to share the pain of loss with the one who is not chosen. The aunt, in my opinion, shows this kind of sensitivity in her decisions.)

Natalie's aunt is far from being a scrupulous person. Scrupulosity consists mainly in never being satisfied that one has made a reasonably sound decision; the scrupulous person wavers about decisions already made, continually questions his own sincerity to make a decision, or the competence of the person advising him, or the principles on which his own or his adviser's decisions are based. He remains scrupulous as long as he wavers and never comes to any conviction about his intention. This frame of mind is different from a state of doubt about whether one has acted rightly. A person may not be absolutely sure that he has

5   Ibid., p. 179.

chosen the right course, but if he is faced with the need to choose, he has the strength to make a decision and commit himself to it until such time as new evidence arises which throws a substantially different light on his choice—in which case he is ready to reconsider the validity of his decision. The scrupulous person, on the other hand, is one who keeps returning over the same evidence without being able to form a stable judgment about it, i.e., without arriving at any moral commitment.

Looked at closely, the aunt's behaviour has none of the marks of this scrupulosity. Her hesitations belong to the period of deliberation in which the person gives himself time to weigh up all the possibilities and to view the situation from all sides. Without this 'discussion', no mature moral judgment is likely to be arrived at—at least in most cases. Once she has deliberated, the aunt's decision is definite and unwavering, and she acts in conformity with her decision. These are the marks of a moral person, whereas the compromising, wavering scrupulous person is essentially unmoral, is incapable both of morality and of immorality.

One tidy aspect of the aunt's attitude is that she does not indulge in moral commentaries on behaviour. The *Confession* is not moralistic in tone. The sentimentalist loves to moralize as a compensation for not committing himself to a concrete course of moral action.[6] The aunt is extremely sparing of moral reflections; she limits herself to explaining how the conflict between herself and Narziss arose. This is mature analysis which recognizes the presence of two different sets of values and shows the complexity that arose from the fact that the aunt herself could not in conscience yield to Narziss' more flexible conception. The more serious problem in the situation was due not so much to the aunt's strict attitude but to the lack of openness on Narziss' part: he pretended to admire her for her convictions, but at the same time tried, indirectly, to break down her defences. The fair conclusion in such a situation is that the relationship broke down not because of any ethical narrowness on the aunt's part or ethical laxity on Narziss' part; the relationship did not depend directly on ethical questions, but rather on Narziss' lack of openness which prevented a clear confrontation of views and the possibility of finding a solution to their problems. Natalie's comment about the aunt's anxiety could easily seem to refer to this problem; there is little else in the *Confession* that it could refer to. Yet close examination of the text will show that a deep relationship between the aunt and Narziss was not possible because Narziss was too devious.[7] Under the circumstances we can only admire the aunt's insight, judgment and decisiveness.

A further characteristic of the sentimental person that, reading

---

6 Ibid.

7 See below, chapter 7.

Natalie's criticism of the aunt, we would expect to find in the *Confession*, is that of a negative outlook on life. Wieser calls this 'ressentiment'.[8] It is the negative attitude of a person who is disillusioned with the world around him and can find little to praise in it. The attitude is the reverse side of the moralizer's character and it is equally foreign to the aunt's make-up. Her eventual withdrawal from the round of social engagements which once preoccupied her was due not to a condemnation of these things in themselves, but to the undesirable effect they were having on her. Far from condemning these things and the people who participate in them, she gave her own (temporary) lack of freedom as the reason for withdrawing from them.[9] Eventually she did feel free with regard to them because she had achieved an inner liberation that helped her to move freely amongst all of creation. They were not bad; she had been incapable, for a time, of free involvement with them. Her recognition and admission of this fact shows anything but an attitude of 'ressentiment'.

Similarly, in her criticism of the religious attitudes of her acquaintances: there is no suggestion of contempt at their limited vision; she says outright that they were often merely gnawing at the shell while she was convinced she enjoyed the kernel of religion.[10] A psycho-analyst who has experienced a growth towards inner unity in himself will also be well aware of the fears and illusions that many another person still suffers from (though the persons themselves may not be aware of the truth of their own situation). His accurate judgment about his own healthy inner state and about their entangled one says nothing about the psycho-analyst being a self-righteous person. Such judgments are possible, and a person can be entitled to make them without deserving the stigma of self-righteousness. In the same way we have no reason, from the aunt's comments, to suppose that her criticism of the primitive religious attitudes she sees around her (and which she had once to some extent shared) are based on any self-righteous or negatively critical frame of mind. Analysis of her own inner progress, quite justifiable in itself, justifies her critical comments as illustrations of what inner states she has left behind her.[11]

Towards the end of the *Confession*, she criticizes her uncle and the other educators; but this is again not done in any purely negative spirit; it is rather her attempt to defend her own values and the contribution she could have made to the education of her nieces and nephew had she not

8 *Der sentimentale Mensch,* p. 7.
9 *Lehrjahre,* p. 378, 31ff.
10 Ibid., p. 396, 31.
11 Ibid., p. 395.

been out-manoeuvred by her uncle and his associates.[12] Her state of health and her relatively dependent position in the family made it easy for the uncle to shield the children from her, so as to limit the influence her religious attitude would have on them. A sentimental response would have been not to react at all and merely to dwell on the feeling of rejection. But the aunt does not enjoy martyrdom for its own sake. A different sentimental reaction would have been to demolish others' positive contributions—the attitude of 'ressentiment'. But with the aunt the accent is on defending what her own contribution would be if she had not been outflanked by others who had a more favourable position of influence.

---

12   Ibid., pp. 419f.

3
Relationship to Pietism

To complete our introductory comments we need to relate—again in a general way—the experience of this 'schöne Seele' to the pietist movement. As already mentioned, it is highly unlikely that Goethe borrowed the expression 'schöne Seele' from the pietist movement. Yet there is much to suggest that the experience of this particular 'schöne Seele' is a typically pietist one.

August Langen is the leading authority on pietism amongst the philologists. Like the other philologists he admits: 'We do not know whether and to what extent this portrait is based on authentic writings of the model, Susanna von Klettenberg'.[1] But despite this, when compiling his *Wortschatz des deutschen Pietismus* he has no hesitation in drawing on the *Confession* as an authentic pietist document—for the following reason: the theme of the *Confession* is typically pietist, namely, the journey of the individual soul from the world to God.[2] But not only is the theme a pietist one: as is to be expected, the language reflects the pietist world of experience: 'So we find . . . expressions like: God is a confidant and friend of the soul, the soul as mirror of God; further, (God as) "base" of the heart, seek for God, find Him, speak with Him, intercourse with God, open to or closed off from God, the influence and impression of God, guidance and attraction, being touched, distracted, recollected, quiet; inwardness, tendency, peace of soul, to soar up to God, wings, empty, frivolous piety and so on. Here there is, on the whole, an abundance of pietist terms which, if Goethe did not have an autobiography of the heroine before him, show at any rate an astoundingly good knowledge of pietist terminology'.[3]

---

1 Langen, *Wortschatz des deutschen Pietismus*, p. 465.
2 Ibid.
3 Ibid.

Susanna von Klettenberg was beyond all doubt a pietist, which means that if the document is substantially hers it is pietist through and through. Working, however, on the more likely assumption that it stems substantially from Goethe, we still have the assurance that the theme and language of the *Confession* are typically pietist.

Before trying to explain, at least in general terms, the relationship of the *Confession* to the pietist movement in Goethe's day, it would be well to describe the context.

Pietism is a movement which grew up in the Lutheran Church as a reaction against a stagnant orthodoxy. It had its roots in various mystical traditions going back as far as St Augustine. Some of the main figures in this line were Gregory of Nyssa, Bonaventure, Tauler, Bernard of Clairvaux and the author of the *Imitation of Christ* (long thought to be Thomas a'Kempis). Augustine was of special importance both for his pessimistic conception of human nature and for the vital character of his religious experience. Bernard's stress on the love relationship between Jesus and the Christian soul, his cult of Christ's wounds, and the spouse imagery all had an important influence on the pietist movement. Of the German medieval mystics (Eckhardt, Seuse and Tauler) Tauler seemed to have had the greatest influence.[4]

The Spanish mystical tradition of the sixteenth century, of which St Teresa of Avila and St John of the Cross are the outstanding representatives, had a far-reaching influence in Europe in the seventeenth and eighteenth centuries and left its mark on the pietist movement. Its effect is consolidated by the influence of the Quietism of Michael de Molinos (1640-1696), Pierre Poiret (1646-1719) and Mme Guyon (1648-1717). In Calvinist Holland there was the example of the revivalist sects and the separatism of de Labadie (1610-1674). Specifically German influences were that of the mystics and theosophists Sebastian Franck, Valentin Weigel and Caspar Schwenkfeld in the sixteenth century and, in the seventeenth century, Daniel Sudermann (1550-1631) and Angelus Silesius (1624-1677).[5]

In the Lutheran Church, Johannes Arndt (1555-1621), with his *Four Books of True Christianity* (1605-1610), became an important forerunner of pietist devotion. But Philipp Jakob Spener (1635-1705), the author of *Pia Desideria*, is the real founder of pietism. In dealing with a religious movement which allows of considerable variation in doctrine and concrete living, we are perhaps best advised to centre our brief résumé of the movement on figures like Spener himself, August Hermann Francke (1663-1727) and Count Zinzendorf (1700-1766) who

4   See August Langen, *'Pietismus'*. In *Reallexikon der deutschen Literaturgeschichte*, vol. 3 (1966), p. 106.

5   Ibid.

are its acknowledged leaders. In reacting against the dry scholasticism of the Lutheran preachers, Spener stressed the need for preaching that not merely instructed people but exerted a profound influence on their lives. Elite groups were soon formed (collegia pietatis) whose aim was not to revolt against the orthodox Lutheran Church by breaking with it but to reform and enliven it from within. In this the pietist tendency differs from the Separatism of the various minorities who chose to break with the established Church—whether Lutheran, Calvinist or Anglican.[6]

By 1691 Spener had gained a position of influence in Berlin. The year 1694 saw the foundation of the University of Halle and from there the influence of pietism spread far and wide. Francke continued the work of Spener, stressing missionary activity, education and social work.

Count Zinzendorf's contribution marks a further stage in the development of pietism. He laid stress both on personal experience in religion and on commitment to a community—with, as the basis of both, a glowing love expressed often in highly erotic terms. The community of Moravian Brethren at Herrnhut, under the guidance of their bishop (Zinzendorf himself), achieved a unified, vibrant community life and furthered the development of missionary activity.[7]

In the reformed Churches important exponents of pietism were Tersteegen (1697-1769), a significant poet; Lavater (1741-1801), the Calvinist pastor in Zürich (who through his correspondence and discussions had an important influence on the early Goethe); and Jung-Stilling (1740-1817) (whom Goethe had met in Strasbourg in 1770).[8]

As H. R. G. Günther says:

> German pietism is a late offshoot of the great mystical movement which began in the last decade of the seventeenth century on Calvinist territory: it made English Puritanism and Dutch Precisism its intellectual centre and it proceeded to flood western Europe and America. This religious mass movement was consciously international or rather: supranational; and yet in each nation and each individual believer it takes on its own personal form and content. This is a clear sign that it reaches right down to the metaphysical depths of human existence.[9]

Thus pietism has its roots in a profound and widespread mystical movement, which accounts for the clear emphasis on inner experience found in pietist documents in general and in the *Confession* in particular.

Günther traces the cult of the inner life (Innerlichkeit), which charac-

---

6 See Cragg, *The Church and the Age of Reason*, p. 105.
7 Ibid., p. 103.
8 *'Pietismus'*, p. 105.
9 Günther, *Psychologie des Pietismus*, pp. 146f.

terizes the general mystical movement, back as far as St Augustine whose emphasis on inner experience stood out in contrast to the Greek tendency to accept and contemplate an ordered external cosmos with its divinely given set of laws. The Augustinian emphasis broke forth again with the Reformation, then with the Jansenists in Port Royal, and a third time with the pietist movement in the (late) seventeenth and eighteenth centuries.[10]

Along·with the cult of the inner life that characterizes these three more modern movements, we find another trait they share—one which perhaps again betrays its origin in the Augustinian spirituality. Despite the fact of his conflict with the Manichees, Augustine's philosophy and theology reflect a radical distrust of human nature, and when the Reformers (Luther and Calvin) take the Pauline doctrine about original sin to mean that, after the fall, human nature was radically and intrinsically spoiled, they do not significantly differ from Augustine's own position on the subject. (Luther was an Augustinian Friar.) A similarly pessimistic view is repeated in the Jansenist movement in the seventeenth century.

German pietism, which grew up in the midst of the Lutheran church, belongs in the same pessimistic tradition under discussion. Spener and Francke were convinced that human nature was radically evil as a result of original sin, and they considered that genuine religious experience had to begin with a deep conviction of one's own sinfulness. Conversion followed on this experience. Contrition for one's own sinfulness resulted in pain and sorrow for sin. Penitential exercises were undertaken as a means of producing feelings of sorrow, feelings of pain for having sinned. The purpose was to bring about a rebirth, a changed way of life. Feelings were deliberately aroused for ethical purposes. A later development of pietism is marked by a shift of emphasis in this regard: Francke's followers seem to have misunderstood him and eventually to have sought to arouse feelings of sorrow for sin just for the sake of the feelings themselves. In this way they became forerunners of sentimentalism in Germany.[11]

This basic attitude towards original sin is accompanied by other attitudes which become characteristic of German pietism. The conviction that no good can come from one's own sinful desires requires the abnegation of one's own will in favour of the divine will. The criterion that one is acting according to God's will is that one acts in diametrical opposition to one's own will which, because of original sin, is necessarily bad.[12] The attitude of calmness (Gelassenheit) is based on the

10   Ibid., p. 148.
11   Ibid., p. 167.
12   Ibid., p. 157.

assurance that one lives not according to one's own will, but precisely against one's own desires which have been countered and replaced by God's will.

Correspondingly, if the person's own will has been eliminated because bad and misleading, he is thrown back on the divinity. He does not shape his own life and map out a course of good for himself—his spoiled human nature makes this impossible. In so far as he begins to build up a new life after conversion, he is dependent on following the leads God gives him. Hence the supreme importance attached to the role of divine providence.[13] Thus it is typical of pietists to find the finger of God everywhere. They interpret the slightest occurrences as warnings by God that they are embarking on a false venture or as confirmation that they should go ahead. They expect God to guide their development by his direct influence in their lives.

It is not difficult to see how the pietist conviction about God's direct interest in the individual person would tend to heighten the person's awareness of his own special position. This phenomenon, common enough in the history of Christianity, has links in this context with Calvinism. The Calvinist, according to Günther, is on the one hand conscious of himself as the servant, but on the other he is the privileged one in the kingdom of heaven because he is the prophet charged with carrying out God's work on earth.[14] In pietism this self-consciousness developed into an awareness of the immanent value of the self, whereas the person's value in Calvinism was understood more directly in connection with the other world. Characteristic of this immanentist orientation of the pietist attitude is the desire to enjoy directly the experience of reconciliation and union with God,[15] rather than the seemingly more modest desire of the Calvinist to feel assured of salvation as long as he directs his active living to God's glory and excludes all forms of creature-worship. For the Calvinist, experience of bliss in his earthly life is not essential to salvation, whereas for the pietist it is a necessary condition.

The emphasis laid by pietists on feeling and enjoying reconciliation and union with God governs a further emphasis which is typical of the movement: whereas the Calvinist's spirituality had a strongly ethical side, the pietist emphasis on the inner experience of reconciliation with God amounted to a stress laid on mysticism rather than on concrete activity in the external world. Thus, as Günther points out, *love of neighbour*, which when stressed is usually central to a given ethic, was in the case of the pietists largely a means for mirroring one's own per-

---

13   Ibid., p. 158.
14   Ibid., p. 164.
15   Ibid.

fection; it is not the neighbour—the other—on which the pietist focusses, but the self.[16]

A brief consideration of the pietist's relationship to the person of Christ could help highlight some main characteristics of the movement. Redemption, for the pietist, does not consist in the Lutheran act of faith in the miracle of redemption, but only in the direct and profound friendship with the God-Man, Jesus (Herzensverkehr mit dem Gottmenschen Jesus).[17] This attitude represents not only the rejection of any primary role played by dogma in the Catholic sense, but is also a departure from the Lutheran conception of dogma. For the pietist, the intense focus on the person of Christ and the conviction that the divinity does in fact work directly on the individual soul without always using the mediation of the Church and the Bible, helped him to the view that the historical Christ was superfluous, i.e., the Christ seen as founder of a Church intended by God as a means of salvation.[18]

The Moravian Brotherhood founded by Count Zinzendorf was far less interested in understanding the relationship between God and Man in Christ than in centring their religiosity on the individual personality of Christ. With an often jarring sensuality they refer to Christ as the bridegroom, and their own religious experience reflects a disturbing eroticism. A typical example of this influence is found in one of Novalis' *Geistliche Lieder,* where the understandable erotic treatment of the human love theme between man and woman is inextricably bound up with a far less healthy eroticism involving the human person's love for God. In an unmistakably religious context where he is speaking of the divine meaning of the Lord's Supper Novalis says:

> There is no end to the sweet meal
> Love is never sated
> She can never have the beloved
> Inwardly enough, enough to herself
> Her joy advances deeper, nearer
> Transformed by ever tender lips.

> Nie endet das süsse Mahl,
> Nie sättigt die Liebe sich.
> Nicht innig, nicht eigen genug
> Kann sie haben den Geliebten.
> Von immer zärteren Lippen
> Verwandelt wird das Genossene
> Inniglicher und näher.[19]

---

16   Ibid., p. 166.
17   Ibid., p. 172.
18   Ibid., pp. 172f.
19   Novalis, *Schriften,* p. 167.

Perhaps even more striking as a confusion of two different levels of love (one for the divine and one for the human) are the following lines from the same poem:

> Everything is to become body.
> One body,
> The blissful pair swims
> In the divine blood.

> Einst ist alles Leib,
> Ein Leib,
> In himmlischem Blute
> Schwimmt das selige Paar.[20]

Along with this erotic relationship to Christ is found the tendency of the pietist to look on Christ as the Ideal.[21] He sees in himself a parallel to Christ as incarnation of the Godhead: the terrors which the pietist experiences in his conversion—in the realization of his own sinfulness—are an equivalent of Christ's sufferings; and Christ is the Ideal in so far as he forms a contrast to the pietist's own worthlessness; Christ is in fact the other self, the good in the pietist that constitutes his value and forms the basis of his self-esteem. He realizes that this good cannot come from his own being, which he considers totally corrupted by original sin. The pietist aims at identification of himself with the person of Christ. This is the climax of his tendency towards self-glorification: towards his own deification. Without amounting to a claim of absolute identity with the godhead, the pietist tendency was able to produce a Jung-Stilling who was convinced that not only did he have a special role as a person chosen by God but that he was next in order of importance after Christ Himself.[22]

The outline given here should be sufficient to help us compare and contrast the book of the *Confession* with the experience that is typical of pietism. The points we have just discussed—concerning the pietist attitude towards inner experience, original sin, conversion, calmness, providence, ethics, feeling of bliss, love of neighbour, individualism and relationship to Christ—give us the points of comparison we require for a preliminary evaluation of the extent to which the aunt is typically pietist.

The *Confession* as a form of limited autobiography is typical of the pietist preoccupation with self (though the mere fact of its being an autobiography does not necessarily identify it with pietism, even in the

---

20 Ibid.
21 Günther, *Psychologie des Pietismus*, p. 172.
22 Günther, *Jung-Stilling*, p. 91.

eighteenth century). In pietism the awareness of privilege in religious experience gave rise to innumerable 'confessions'. These contained, as in the case of Goethe's *Confession*, careful analysis of the person's own inner experience. Thus, the aunt's self-analysis is typically pietist in that she interprets, above all, her own inner growth and the development of her inner relationship to God. This is the point of view from which the *Confession* is written, rather than any which would tend to relate her own life to the social, political and cultural situation of her time. (With regard to the aunt, we have no reason to suspect that there was, in any case, much of consequence in her life apart from the religious aspect.)

The preoccupation in the *Confession* with inner experience and the growing confidence the aunt shows in evidence drawn from this source puts her in the tradition that Günther traces from St Augustine through the Reformation, Jansenism and pietism.[23] But it is perhaps first in her attitude towards sin that we begin to suspect a deviation from the pietist pattern. She expressly says that she does not agree with the Halle conversion method. For ten years she had been preoccupied with her religious experience and never knew what was meant by sin. This was directly opposed to the Halle 'system', according to which at the outset of any profound religious development the experience of one's own sinfulness is essential. It is true that the aunt eventually does gain an awareness of sin which makes her realize what faith means—the total turning of the person towards Christ the Redeemer. But even here she speaks of her potentiality for sin in a way which smacks more of a mild Catholic interpretation of original sin as a proneness to sin rather than a radical corruption of the person; and even though she says that this experience of sin brought her a completely new kind of religious experience, she realizes afterwards that it is not really a difference of kind but rather one of intensity and duration.[24] The deepening and strengthening of her religious experience through the experience of sin does not allow us to point to a typically pietist religiosity. Because of the continuity of this 'new' experience with an experience that had grown organically over a period of ten years—in which sin was seen as a lack of freedom but not as a radical evil in the person—the aunt's experience is more reasonably interpreted as a deviation from the normal pietist pattern.

Such a deviation may be taken as a sign of Goethe's own hand shaping the narrative. In comparison with the main stream of pietist literature, the *Confession* tones down what is usually a strong emphasis. Goethe himself was eventually repulsed by pietism for its insis-

---

23   Günther, *Psychologie des Pietismus*, p. 148.

24   *Lehrjahre*, p. 395.

tence on the ravages of original sin in the human person. As he explains in *Dichtung und Wahrheit*, he never felt fully accepted in pietist circles and this was due to the contrast between his optimistic and their pessimistic view of human nature.[25] After his contact with the pietists in Strasbourg in 1770-1771—he found them too gloomy for him at a time when his friendship with Herder and love for Friederike Brion were awakening him to a highly optimistic conception of life—his relations with the movement were strained; and although Susanna von Klettenberg remained a close and highly esteemed friend (until her death in 1774), he continued to drift away from pietism. Before pietism could play the positive role required of it in his novel, Goethe had to prune back certain undesirable aspects. The chief one of these was clearly the negative view of human nature connected with original sin. When, in a letter to Schiller Goethe says, with reference to the inclusion of the *Confession*, that he has 'sailed safely past the rocks', this is apparently what he means.[26]

But there are other modifications based on this first one. The 'schöne Seele's' 'Gelassenheit', or calmness, is not based on the pietist choice of a course of action which is diametrically opposed to one's own will. Her criterion that she is acting according to the divine will is not the absolute abandonment of her own will but the inner experience that the object of her potential choice harmonizes (or not) with the basic experience of serenity and peace she enjoys in her relationship to God. If the harmony set up by her fundamental experience of relationship to the divine is not disturbed by what she experiences of the new object of her choice, then she can be assured she is right in her choice: if the harmony is disturbed, then she knows she is wrong. In the case of the 'schöne Seele', the 'Gelassenheit' is not purely a product of self-negation, but of the fundamental relationship to God, which is primarily something positive.

Correspondingly, the aunt's attitude to Providence is different from that of the typical pietist. Having an inner criterion at her disposal— the inner awareness of her relationship to God and the peace and calmness that result from it—she has no need to resort to outer signs that God is pointing her this way or that. The pietists' radical mistrust of self led them to seek all kinds of confirmation that God's influence was at work. Hence the continual interpretation of the smallest occurrences as indications that God was pleased or displeased with a particular course of action chosen. They saw His Providence at work in all the outward circumstances surrounding their lives. The 'schöne Seele' herself is conscious of the need for scepticism in this regard. (The

---

25   *Dichtung und Wahrheit*, vol. 3, p. 15.

26   18 August 1795.

danger of complete subjectivism in interpreting the divine significance of trivial external events is apparent.) She disturbed the people who, in trying to prove God's interest in them, cited instances of prayers that had been answered. Whereas the pietists fastened onto the slightest 'proof' of this kind,[27] the aunt's conviction was based on the global experience of God's presence to her. Not a limited series of isolated instances, but the totality of manifestations bolstered her conviction:

> How happy I was that a thousand small events conspired to prove, with as much certainty as that my breathing is a sign that I am alive, that God is with me in the world. He was near to me, I was in His presence.

> Wie glücklich war ich, dass tausend kleine Vorgänge zusammen, so gewiss als das Atemholen Zeichen meines Lebens ist, mir bewiesen, dass ich nicht ohne Gott auf der Welt sei! Er war mir nahe, ich war vor ihm.[28]

The conviction resulting from the 'tausend kleine Vorgänge' has as its object God's reality and presence in her life, not His approval or disapproval of any course of action she has determined to follow. Thus she is not looking primarily for divine manifestations to justify what she does; rather, she is becoming continually more aware of God's presence everywhere. The pietist, with the former of these two attitudes, is easily suspected of a self-centred grasping for security; the latter, the attitude of the 'schöne Seele', is a religious awareness of God's presence deserving far less scepticism on our part.

The highly developed self-consciousness of the Calvinist and also of the pietist are found in the aunt, but in a very mild form. The extremes are lacking: she does not see herself as the servant and slave, because the depths of humiliation resulting from the radical conception of original sin are lacking. Her humility and awareness of sin are not the most striking characteristics of her spirituality, though they have their due place. But, lacking this extreme of humility, she at the same time avoids the other extreme of self-exaltation typical both of the Calvinists and of the pietists (see Jung-Stilling whom we mentioned above.) She considers herself favoured by God who has shown her His friendship and led her to a genuine spirituality, whereas others go through the motions of an external religion without penetrating to what she calls the truth (das Wahre). While this is far from the exalted stance taken by the pietists, it is still above the purely superficial level

---

27 *Lehrjahre*, p. 387, 25.
28 Ibid., 37.

of religious experience found in numerous Christian circles. What lifted the aunt above these is the penetration and depth of her experience which became the basis for the major decisions concerning her life, as we shall see in our analysis of the text itself.

Apropos of the fact that the pietist wanted, above all, enjoyment of the experience of reconciliation with God rather than being content, like the Calvinist, with a life led in God's service: the aunt clearly does enjoy the experience of God's friendship, and thus enjoys an equivalent to reconciliation with God. But we have no reason to think that she fastens onto this enjoyment for its own sake, in such a way as to reduce religious experience to a mere source of satisfaction. There is nothing wrong with finding satisfaction in religious experience any more than there is in finding satisfaction in friendship—as long as the other person and the friendship itself are prized rather than one's own personal satisfaction and gain. From this point of view, the aunt's attitude seems to be perfectly healthy.

Her attitude towards the 'beloved ones'[29] is not typical of the pietist. Unlike them, she does not regale us with innumerable good deeds she performed out of love for her 'neighbour'. When she speaks of her contribution to the work in the house, this is not related for its own sake, but merely as an example of the strains that helped undermine her health and that helped her grow in reliance on God. She makes no secret of the fact that she has never been drawn to personal commitment to people outside a limited circle. Unlike her niece Natalie, she would, according to her own words, tend more to buy herself free by gifts of money than to involve herself personally with others in need. In relating this about herself, she is much more sober than the typical pietist who would be caught up in a programme of doing good—in the self-centred attempt to build up esteem for himself in others' eyes and eventually in his own eyes. The pietist's attitude would be thinly veiled, even from himself, but it would nonetheless be part of his very real quest of self-exaltation.

The aunt had in common with the pietists their intense focussing on the person of Christ. Her profound experience of faith was directly linked with Christ the Redeemer as was typical of orthodox Lutheran spirituality; but like the pietists, the foundation of all her spirituality was the profound friendship (Herzensverkehr) with God and, as time went on, more specifically with the God-Man, Christ. Though she experiences this relationship to Christ in terms of bride-mysticism— which, as we have seen, has a long Christian tradition—she avoids an extreme and suspect eroticism which was found in the Zinzendorf brand of pietism.

---

29   In the original German text this extract appears in English.

The aunt knew and appreciated Count Zinzendorf's spirituality. She found that his verses, hymns and prayers were genuine and expressed what she herself was experiencing; but there was a certain tendency to ornament the central experience by the cult of devout practices; the aunt was critical of these, though she took part in them herself and found some meaning in them. The danger was that they could prove very distracting from the central religious experience itself, and eventually she gave them up. Though attracted to the Count and the Moravian Brethren, she never actually joined them. She remained an independent Moravian Sister (eine herrnhutische Schwester auf meine eigene Hand).[30]

The 'schöne Seele' of the *Confession* belongs in the broad pietist stream of religious experience. As we saw in the beginning of this section, pietism is difficult to define because it admits of the most varied manifestations. But the characteristics we have outlined above are sufficient to delineate the pietist movement; and, as we have just seen, the *schöne Seele* manifests these characteristics; just the same, we need to notice some strong modifications of the normal pietist pattern of experience, so that when we refer to her as a pietist we are conscious of the qualifications contained in the designation.

---

30 *Lehrjahre*, p. 398, 20.

4
On the Analysis of the Confession

Having attempted to relate, in a general way, the aunt's experience to the sentimentalism and pietism of the eighteenth century, we can now proceed to a detailed analysis of the *Confession*. The central aim of this study is to focus on particular aspects of the religious experience reflected in this book. One of the immediate results of the study should be a clearer view of the religious phenomenon (or the phenomenon of transcending foreground experience) than has been offered us so far in studies of Goethe's novel. In so far as we seek to analyse and draw attention to a certain constant structure in the religious experience of the aunt, Natalie and Wilhelm, our investigation is philosophical—it amounts to a type of existential analysis. It is philosophical also from another point of view: namely, that it seeks to indicate a method of approaching literary works in which the religious phenomenon undoubtedly plays some sort of role.

From a further point of view, the study belongs to the realm of literary criticism. F. R. Leavis, in his essay on 'Criticism and Philosophy', says:

> The business of the literary critic is to attain a peculiar completeness of response and to observe a peculiarly strict relevance in developing his response into commentary; he must be on his guard against abstracting improperly from what is in front of him and against any premature or irrelevant generalizing—of it or from it. His first concern is to enter into possession of the given poem (let us say) in its concrete fullness, and his constant concern is never to lose his completeness of possession, but rather to increase it.[1]

Our aim is to focus on elements of the novel which will add to the 'completeness of response' and, equally, to avoid 'abstracting im-

---

1   F. R. Leavis, *The Common Pursuit* (London 1966), p. 213.

properly' from what is in front of us. A method of approach (to a literary text) that lets the lived religious experience show itself—and does not merely use the text as a point of departure for speculations —is philosophical, because phenomenological in its treatment of religious experience; and it can also simultaneously be a method of literary criticism because, in guarding against abstraction and generalizing, it strives to 'enter into possession' of the given work 'in its concrete fullness'. Our 'constant concern is never to lose . . . completeness of possession, but rather to increase it'.

The danger of confusing philosophy and literary criticism is apparent. This imposes on us the task not only of appreciating what divides them, but also of seeing where they overlap. This latter task has become all the more urgent in modern times where philosophy, in its phenomenological, existential and personalist trends, does not fly off so readily into abstractions but dwells on and stays with what is concretely experienced. If the concretely experienced that the philosopher dwells on is embodied in a literary work—for example a novel like the *Apprenticeship*—then it is obvious that the work of a philosopher and a literary critic must to a large extent overlap, for they are both interested in the life of the novel which is a large part of its 'concrete fullness'.

In this context, the word 'life' is not meant to connote the vital forces resulting from the human person's deep roots in biological reality; nor does it refer to spontaneity as opposed to culture and form; rather, it refers to the whole range of personal experience which it is possible to portray in a literary work. Taken in this sense, the 'life' of the novel is human experience so convincingly portrayed that the reader is made to feel he is confronted with genuine human experience, i.e., of a kind that reflects the total complexity and depth of our existence. 'Life' exists in the novel if a live experience of human existence is communicated to the reader. It is this kind of life that interests both philosopher and critic.

A pitfall for the philosopher undertaking what amounts to a twofold task is that he runs the risk of treating a novel as a book of philosophy, which it is not. If he treats it as the phenomenon which it is, on the other hand, he must be prepared (and equipped) to respond constantly to the novel in the way a literary critic does. The life of the novel reveals itself through language which must be read the way an 'artist' reads—not the way philosophers, historians or sociologists as such are trained to read.

The pattern of responses demanded is quite complex. At the risk of subjecting the work to a purely exterior treatment which either violates or, at any rate, uses it unauthentically, the philosopher needs to remain constantly aware of the fact that he is moving not only in the domain of philosophy, but just as much in that of literary criticism. He must be prepared to meet the two sets of demands.

Although it will be necessary in evaluating the significance of the aunt's experience to begin by examining (in chapter 5) what various people in the novel say about her, the real evaluation will come in our further chapters, which have as their aim to reveal the life that goes on in the aunt—i.e., the life springing from her religious experience. We shall see, for instance, the constant recurrence of motifs like 'cheerfulness', 'strength', 'joy', 'freedom', 'inner harmony', 'ability to make decisions', 'independence of judgment', all of which grow in proportion as her religious experience deepens and intensifies.

The aunt's religious experience can, as we shall see, aptly be described as the transcending of the concrete foreground of experience to the background aspect which for her is just as real. It will become apparent that transcending does not mean leaving the foreground aspect behind, but moving in the foreground in such a way as to remain open and free for an increasingly fuller awareness of the background.

There are two terms here that require clarification: 'transcendence' and 'experience'.

With reference to Goethe the term 'transcendence' has to be used cautiously. At the time of writing the *Apprenticeship* Goethe was at the classical stage of his evolution. By this time he had achieved, by contrast to his earlier *Sturm und Drang* period, both an inner equilibrium and an equilibrium between himself and the outside world. In accepting his role as a statesman at the court of the duke Karl August in Weimar, he had shown his capacity to set limits to an unconditioned striving that would otherwise have dissociated his interest from the real, concrete world. He came to terms with concrete reality and, by imposing stern limits on himself, he opted to live in the present instead of, for example, the past or the future or—by a form of transcending—in a world entirely other than the concrete one of which we have direct experience. Goethe opted for life in this world; this means that we must exercise caution if speaking, in his regard, of transcendence.

Even in the case of Natalie's aunt, whose experience we cannot simply identify with Goethe's (whatever relationship we eventually decide exists between them), transcendence does not mean merely preoccupation with *another* world. We can use the term to refer to her own experience of 'transcending' the concrete world or we can use it with reference to the other world as a transcendent one. In the first case we soon become aware that transcending the concrete world does not mean leaving it behind her; the Narziss episode, for example, shows transcendence in immanence: i.e., that precisely in her encoun-

ter with the concrete world (Narziss, in this instance) she is able to
attain to a further dimension of reality; this is transcendence that does
not presuppose relinquishing the concrete. In the second case, transcendence refers to a sphere of reality which is not simply reducible to
the everyday concrete world, and yet, in so far as it penetrates into
the latter, becomes to this extent immanent. Transcendence in both of
these cases implies simultaneously some degree of immanence.

The degree to which the transcendent sphere becomes immanent is
the measure of the possibility of the human person's having experience
of the transcendent. In the context of this study, the word 'experience'
is not meant to imply any manipulation or exploitation of the transcendent, as if examining it closely would lead to knowledge giving us
power over it. 'Experience' in our context is not a process by which
we can eventually reduce the 'other' to readily comprehensible structures which would make its influence more predictable. Instead,
'experience' refers to the person's awareness of contact with the transcendent (in so far as it becomes immanent) and awareness of the effect
produced on the person's own inner life as a result of this contact.
Thus, when we speak here of transcendent experience, we are referring first and foremost to the person's own transcendence of the purely
concrete foreground world (which is the ordinary everyday object of
normal experience) by becoming aware of his contact with a further
transcendent sphere. According to what we have defined as experience,
in his transcendent experience he becomes aware of contact with the
transcendent sphere and of the various effects this contact brings about
in his inner life: the joy, strength, liberty and interior harmony mentioned above.

The basic experience of joy means for Natalie's aunt the sense of
fulfilment based on her new awareness that existence has profound
meaning and value. This awareness is a direct result of her experience
of contact with the transcendent sphere, and expresses itself in an attitude of gaiety. Her strength comes from her awareness that her life
is in the hands of this superior transcendent force which her experience
leads her to trust; this strength is, again, the basis of her independence
of judgment and capacity to make her own decisions. When the foreground and background aspects of her experience fuse in such a way as
to produce no conflict the outcome, psychologically, is a concomitant
experience of harmony within herself and harmony of herself with the
universe; this is an awareness of a healthy orientation of her inner life
in involvement with the exterior world of persons and things.

The experience of harmony is produced by and is a symptom of an
inner freedom she has won. The fusing of the foreground and background presupposes a basic freedom with regard to the concrete foreground world (of persons and things). Once involvement with the

background element has become complete and radical, the person is able to see the foreground in proper perspective and thus become free in regard to it.

But this is above all freedom in involvement, not the kind of freedom that ignores that in regard to which it is free. She does not have to escape, in order to be free, but because of the security arising from her rootedness in the background sphere she is independent in her involvement in the foreground and has no need to grasp at what lies in the foreground. Two components of her freedom are: firstly, her otherness and, secondly, her fulfilment. The otherness means her profound relationship to the background aspect of her experience in so far as this relationship puts her beyond the control of forces (personal or otherwise) that might seek to gain mastery over her; this gives her protection in her passivity and exposure to the concrete world. Her fulfilment means her profound relationship to the background in so far as this relationship puts her beyond the need of grasping at persons and objects to fill a radical vacuum in her life. Her basic fulfilment (through contact with the background element) can well leave her with the deep desire for further fulfilment in the foreground sphere, but protects her against becoming a slave to her own desire (her activity with regard to the foreground world).

It is our contention here that the aunt's own experience has not been appreciated in its fullness. Thus the present analysis of her experience is aimed at establishing the basis for a more accurate and more profound appreciation both of the aunt as a character in the novel and of the 'schöne Seele' as a Goethean phenomenon; it could also serve as the basis for a detailed comparison between this particular 'schöne Seele' and others like Natalie, or, earlier, Iphigenie and the Princess (in *Tasso*).

Put in general terms, the method functions in the following way: in a first reading of the novel, one experiences one's own spontaneous reactions to the novel; at this stage it may not at all be clear what one is reacting to, but on a second reading one begins to focus on the aspects which were alive from the beginning. One notes the particular passages where the impression is noticeably strong and begins to relate them to one another. As one's grasp of the whole novel grows, these particular aspects are better understood and their significance for the novel as a whole is better appreciated. Amongst the related passages themselves, one discovers deeper and deeper links, some of which are consciously contrived by the author himself. They belong to the level of manifest content of the novel, reflecting the author's conscious shaping of his artistic work.

Other links—the structural elements common to the experience of various characters in the novel (for example, the aunt, Natalie, and

Wilhelm)—belong to the latent content of the novel. (Paradoxical though it may seem: even though these latter links are valid and, as will be shown, relevant to literary criticism, Goethe himself need not have been the slightest bit aware of them. The function of the novelist is different from that of the critic. The novel is the life produced and shaped by the novelist. His final responsibility is not to explain the links and inner workings of the novel but to create them. Goethe would be the last one to claim that he had an exhaustive knowledge of what was happening in the *Apprenticeship*. A sign of the novel's greatness is that neither Goethe himself nor any critic has said the last word about it. The task of the critics will be to let their own experience lead them to the discovery of new dimensions in the experience reflected in the novel. There is need for caution here if distortion is to be avoided.) It is this latent content which we shall explore, attempting to reach it through the level of manifest content, where Goethe's shaping hand—serving his classical 'Stilwille'—is at work.

In the *Confession*, the structures which are central to our study are not difficult to focus on, because they are close to the thematic surface. With this starting point, we can establish the presence of the structure with some assurance.

5
The Confession *in the Context of the* Apprenticeship

The aunt's role in the novel as a whole becomes clear only after a certain amount of analysis. In the *Apprenticeship,* she is sometimes praised and sometimes sharply criticized. Thus the question arises: to what extent is her experience to be taken seriously?

To answer this question we need, firstly, to clear away the doubts expressed in the novel as to the genuineness of her experience. This task requires a discussion of the opinions expressed in the novel, and these we shall deal with immediately. Secondly, we need to draw attention to the indirect hints given by the author himself that the aunt's experience is basically a healthy one (and therefore acceptable); and this we can do in the course of analysing her experience. But, thirdly, the question is most decisively answered by the analysis of her experience.

Before proceeding with the analysis of the aunt's experience we need to clear the way by assessing the value of criticisms directed at her in the novel itself. The doctor who introduces the aunt's *Confession* says:

> that for persons labouring under a chronic and partly incurable disposition, he had always found it a very happy circumstance when they chanced to entertain and cherish in their minds true feelings of religion.

> dass er diejenigen Personen sehr glücklich gefunden habe, die bei einer nicht ganz herzustellenden kränklichen Anlage wahrhaft religiöse Gesinnungen bei sich zu nähren bestimmt gewesen wären.[1]

Though imbedded in a context in which the aunt is praised, the linking of her religious experience with her delicate constitution cautions

---

1 *Lehrjahre,* p. 349, 35ff.

reserve—especially in a novel where health and life play such an important role as in the *Apprenticeship*. (See Goethe's treatment of the 'unhealthy' theme where Mignon and the Harpist are concerned.)

Her sternest critic was, however, her own uncle, her father's brother. She herself complains how he kept the children, her own nieces and nephew, away from her as much as he could. He wanted to protect them against her influence:

> I often take it ill of my uncle that, on this account, he considers me dangerous for the little ones.

> es verdriesst mich oft von dem Oheim, dass er mich deshalb für die Kinder gefährlich hält.[2]

She explains the reason for this attitude. Her uncle, like the other educators in the Tower group, 'sought to keep away from the children everything that could lead them to be preoccupied with themselves and with the invisible, unique and faithful friend' (alles von den Kindern zu entfernen suchen, was sie zu dem Umgange mit sich selbst und mit dem unsichtbaren, einzigen treuen Freunde führen könne).[3] The way she mentions their disapproval of her points to her corresponding disapproval of their attitude. In this she is not alone. Natalie, whose opinions and attitudes are most likely to reflect what Goethe himself thinks healthy, modifies her praise of the uncle when she says to Wilhelm:

> And yet he was obliged to confess that life and breath would almost leave him, if he did not now and then indulge himself, and from time to time allow himself a brief and passionate enjoyment of what he could not always praise and justify. 'It is not my fault', said he, 'if I have not brought my inclinations and my reason into perfect harmony'.

> Und doch musste er selbst gestehen, dass ihm gleichsam Leben und Atem ausgehen würde, wenn er sich nicht von Zeit zu Zeit nachsähe und sich erlaubte, das mit Leidenschaft zu geniessen, was er eben nicht immer loben und entschuldigen konnte. 'Meine Schuld ist es nicht', sagte er, 'wenn ich meine Triebe und meine Vernunft nicht völlig habe in Einstimmung bringen können'.[4]

This admission of inconsistency on the uncle's part suggests that, despite all his culture, it would be easy for him to misunderstand his

---

2   Ibid., p. 419, 36ff.

3   Ibid., 34ff.

4   Ibid., p. 539, 23ff.

niece (the aunt of the *Confession*). He himself lacked the inner unity that was central to her experience. Yet he does seem to have appreciated something of her excellence. With a touch of real sympathy he says to her:

> 'You, my dear niece, have, it may be, chosen the better part; you have striven to bring your moral being, your deep, loving nature into harmony with itself and with the supreme being'.

> Sie, liebe Nichte, haben vielleicht das beste Teil erwählt; Sie haben Ihr sittliches Wesen, Ihre tiefe, liebevolle Natur mit sich selbst und mit dem höchsten Wesen übereinstimmend zu machen gesucht . . . .[5]

Perhaps it is just another expression of his inconsistency that he keeps the children away from a person who, in her life, has chosen, in the uncle's own words 'it may be . . . the better part' (vielleicht das beste Teil).

But it would be unfair to discredit his opinion entirely, for Natalie herself esteems him as an educator. We can take it that the uncle was able to understand Natalie far better than he could his own niece; Natalie's relationship to anything religious was far less obvious than that of the aunt, and it was precisely this aspect of experience that was so foreign to the uncle. But even in Natalie's case, it becomes clear that the uncle did not fully understand her. She attributes the smooth course of her development exclusively to the Abbé.

> 'None but the Abbé seemed to understand me: he made me acquainted with myself, with these wishes, these tendencies, and taught me how to satisfy them suitably'.

> Nur der Abbé schien mich zu verstehen, . . . er machte mich mit mir selbst, mit diesen Wünschen und Neigungen bekannt und lehrte mich sie zweckmässig befriedigen.[6]

This relativizes the importance of the uncle's opinion and shows that his attitude towards his niece far from reflects her real significance in the novel.

In order to complete the picture, we need to mention the clearly expressed evidence in favour of the aunt and the genuineness of her experience. This evidence neutralizes the negative attitude of the group of educators and leaves us free to let the aunt's experience speak for itself. The aim of our analysis will be, in the following chapters, to show the experience for what it is—thus letting it speak for itself.

---

5 Ibid., p. 405, 21ff.
6 Ibid., p. 527, 11ff.

The way the *Confession* is introduced into the novel is significant. The doctor, who is responsible for naming the manuscript the *Confession of a Beautiful Soul*, produces it after he has visited Aurelie. His idea in recommending it is to help Aurelie, who is seriously ill. He expects a real and good effect to be produced by it. He speaks enthusiastically of it to Wilhelm for this reason. In fact, the manuscript does have a deep effect on both Aurelie and Wilhelm, so that the doctor's warm recommendation of the document 'which he had received from the hands of an excellent lady, a friend of his, now dead' (das er aus den Händen einer nunmehr abgeschiedenen vortrefflichen Freundin erhalten habe),[7] receives immediate confirmation. Goethe's opinion becomes clear when he writes, without the slightest suggestion of irony:

> The reader will be able to judge the impression they left when he becomes acquainted with the next book. The violent and stubborn disposition of our poor friend was calmed.

> die Wirkung . . . wird der Leser am besten beurteilen können, wenn er sich mit dem folgenden Buche bekannt gemacht hat. Das heftige und trotzige Wesen unsrer armen Freundin ward auf einmal gelindert.[8]

Aurelie had written a harsh letter to Lothario. Now:

> she took the letter back and wrote another one, as it seemed, in a gentler tone. She likewise begged Wilhelm to console her lover.

> Sie nahm den Brief zurück und schrieb einen andern, wie es schien, in sehr sanfter Stimmung; auch forderte sie Wilhelmen auf, ihren Freund . . . zu trösten.[9]

This interior change brought about by the reading of the manuscript and noted by Goethe himself predisposes us to look for something constructive in the *Confession,* a positive rather than a negative influence.

The effect it had on Wilhelm himself is apparent later in the novel when he is conversing with Natalie about the aunt. Natalie asks: 'You have read the book?' (Sie haben das Heft gelesen?), and he replies: 'Yes, . . . with the greatest sympathy, and not without effect on my whole life' (Ja! . . . mit der grössten Teilnahme und nicht ohne Wirkung auf mein ganzes Leben).[10] He then gives what are in effect the reasons for his enthusiastic reaction:

---

7   Ibid., p. 350, 2ff.
8   Ibid., p. 355, 8ff.
9   Ibid., 11ff.
10 Ibid., 518, 7ff.

What most impressed me in this paper was, if I may term it so, the purity of existence, not only of the writer herself, but of all that lay around her; her independent nature, the impossibility of her admitting anything into her soul which would not harmonize with its own noble loving frame of mind.

Was mir am meisten aus dieser Schrift entgegenleuchtete, war, ich möchte so sagen, die Reinlichkeit des Daseins, nicht allein ihrer selbst, sondern auch alles dessen, was sie umgab, diese Selbständigkeit ihrer Natur und die Unmöglichkeit, etwas in sich aufzunehmen, was mit der edlen, liebevollen Stimmung nicht harmonisch war.[11]

This text contains various positive qualities worth listing:

1 the purity of her existence
2 the capacity to radiate this quality around her
3 the autonomy of her nature
4 her inner harmony
5 her noble frame of mind[12]
6 her loving frame of mind[13]

'Purity of existence' (Reinlichkeit des Daseins) does not refer, in this context, to the aunt's eventual abstinence from a marital relationship nor to any attitude of withdrawal from a contaminating world. Neither of these kinds of 'purity' (Reinlichkeit) would impress Wilhelm. The purity referred to here is, positively, none other than the harmony of the elements comprising the aunt's experience[14] and implies, negatively, the exclusion of any factors that would diminish the resonance of this harmony. It is not just an interior characteristic but results from her inner reaction to the outer world as it confronts her; to create her inner harmony she has to react inwardly in a particular way to the real world around her and, since her harmony is more than mere passive acceptance of outward circumstances, she reacts on the exterior world itself, making adjustments in it so as to shape her

---

11 Ibid., 9ff.

12 It is important for Natalie's aunt to be noble (edel) because it is her influence that prepares Wilhelm for entry into the noble world of Natalie. In what does this nobility (edle Stimmung) consist? Negatively, it consists, as we can judge from the context, in her choice to exclude all that would impair her relationship to the background; positively, it consists in the fact that the background itself is the foundation on which her inner disposition is based.

13 Her loving disposition reminds us that the aunt is a pietist reflecting the influence of Zinzendorf's spirituality, which is characterized by love. But quite apart from the influence of this spirituality, her disposition results above all from the love she shows for the Invisible Friend (which is her way of referring to the background).

14 See above, chapter 4.

world and render it acceptable. The product of this inner and outer adjustment is what makes the aunt's existence attractive to Wilhelm. The classical figure that Wilhelm is to become will want to adjust to his world, belong to it; but he will also want to shape it and leave his own stamp on it. During his transition into Natalie's classical world, he is impressed by the 'schöne Seele's' achievement as foreshadowing what he himself seeks to achieve.

Natalie's opinion is no less enlightening than Wilhelm's. Here it will be sufficient to deal with the opinions she herself openly expresses. She has her reservations, but her overall judgment of the aunt is a favourable one. Natalie says to Wilhelm:

> You should have known this excellent person. I owe her much. A very weak state of health, perhaps too much preoccupation with her own thoughts, and along with this, a moral and religious scrupulosity, prevented her from being to the world what, in other circumstances, she might have become. She was a light that shone on only a few friends, and on me especially.

> Sie hätten diese treffliche Person kennen sollen. Ich bin ihr so viel schuldig. Eine sehr schwache Gesundheit, vielleicht zu viel Beschäftigung mit sich selbst, und dabei eine sittliche und religiöse Ängstlichkeit liessen sie das der Welt nicht sein, was sie unter andern Umständen hätte werden können. Sie war ein Licht, das nur wenigen Freunden und mir besonders leuchtete.[15]

Despite her frailty and, according to Natalie, 'perhaps too much pre-occupation with her own thoughts' (vielleicht zu viel Beschäftigung mit sich selbst), she had remained a light which shone even for Natalie herself.

Lothario's opinion corroborates that of both Wilhelm and Natalie. In praising his sister Natalie, towards the end of the novel, he describes her as a 'schöne Seele' and then compares her with their aunt:

> She deserves the honour of this title more than do many others, more, if I may say so, than our aunt herself who, at the time our good doctor named the manuscript, was the 'schönste Natur' whom we had in our circle.

> Ja sie verdient diesen Ehrennamen vor vielen andern, mehr, wenn ich sagen darf, als unsre edle Tante selbst, die zu der Zeit, als unser guter Arzt jenes Manuskript so rubrizierte, die schönste Natur war, die wir in unserm Kreise kannten.[16]

---

15   *Lehrjahre*, p. 517, 33ff.

16   Ibid., p. 608, 19ff.

To stress Natalie's excellence, he takes the best possible comparison: their aunt; and he transfers the title 'schöne Seele' to Natalie. While this clearly subordinates her, it also clearly implies his great esteem for her.

We can assume that Wilhelm's indirect contact with the aunt is mainly a preparation for his moving into Natalie's sphere. Her implied subordination to Natalie plays a similar role to that of the other women in Wilhelm's experience (for example, Mariane, Philine, the Countess). They are all subordinated to Natalie, but that does not mean they are lost in the past. (See Friedrich's words warning Wilhelm about this—on the very last page of the novel.)

Far from discrediting the aunt, all these positive testimonies should dispose us to take her and her experience seriously. But the decisive 'testimony' will be the analysis of the aunt's experience itself. We lay even more store by this kind of evidence than by that of expressly formulated opinions offered us in the novel.

To avoid the risk of violating the work, we shall follow the lines of organic development as they show themselves quite spontaneously in the novel itself. For our purposes, the *Confession* can be divided into three quite distinct phases:

1 the aunt's development during the years of relatively protected homelife, §§6-7;
2 her increased exposure to outside influences, §§8-9;
3 her increased encounter and involvement with her uncle's world, §§10-11.

6

Sheltered Years

In summing up her situation at the end of the first phase, the aunt refers to whisperings in the neighbourhood about the girl 'who had valued God above her bridegroom' (die Gott mehr schätzte als ihren Bräutigam).[1] This expression hints at a valuable starting point for our investigation of the transcendence phenomenon. In the context of this religious development we shall have to watch for and analyse the relevant data as it arises.

Although the first line of the *Confession* introduces the theme of health—she was for seven years a 'quite healthy child' (ein ganz gesundes Kind)—only three lines later the theme of the aunt's physical frailty is there, and with it the resulting preoccupation with her inner self, which is typical of the *Confession*. In this first of the three phases it is quite striking how often a similar sequence occurs: life, conflict and, as a result of this latter, preoccupation with her inner self, which gradually comes to entail preoccupation with God. This repeated rhythm shows also an inner development: the awareness of the 'Invisible Friend' gradually becomes a constant aspect of her inner experience, and not merely something she is aware of during setbacks. We shall see that precisely this second aspect of her experience becomes the backbone of her life and gives her courage to face difficult situations and decisions. With a view to highlighting this positive point, we shall need to watch for signs of the basically healthy attitude of the aunt; it will become clear that her uncle's negative attitude towards her was mainly a misunderstanding of her qualities and of her experience.

Even the first sickness of the eight-year-old is not to be judged too negatively. It influences the girl's development but there is no sug-

---

1 *Lehrjahre*, p. 383, 19.

gestion of its inwardly handicapping her. The signs are instead positive: '. . . and from that moment my soul became all feeling, all memory' (und in dem Augenblick war meine Seele ganz Empfindung und Gedächtnis).[2] This phrase speaks only of a greater awareness. Similarly, where she speaks of the nine months needed for recuperating,[3] she sees them as the occasion for the unfolding of her mind in the way that was proper to her:

> It appears to me the groundwork of my whole way of thinking was laid, as the first means were then afforded my mind of developing itself in its own manner.

> Während des neunmonatlichen Krankenlagers . . . ward, so wie mich dünkt, der Grund zu meiner ganzen Denkart gelegt, indem meinem Geiste die ersten Hülfsmittel gereicht wurden, sich nach seiner eigenen Art zu entwickeln.[4]

These words contain only the suggestion that the sickness helped her develop along the lines natural for her. This text gives us no reason to suppose that her sickness was to form the basis for a sentimental attitude towards life. Sickness need not lead to an acute introversion that constructs an imaginary world as a compensation for one's relative exclusion from the real world around one. The present passage suggests that sickness gives the aunt the opportunity she needs to concentrate on her interior life and thus develop along the lines dictated by her inner being. This results in her self-discovery, and there is nothing in the passage or in the fact of her sickness to suggest morbidity or any other form of the sentimentalism described above. As a protection against the obvious dangers of such a period of sickness her curiosity for all that surrounds her is kept alive by her parents with dolls, picture-books, nature-cabinet and fairy-tales; birds and animals brought in from hunting trips are shown to her.

As early as this she also has some kind of religious experience: 'There were hours in which I had lively conversation with the Invisible Being' (Ich hatte Stunden, in denen ich mich lebhaft mit dem unsichtbaren Wesen unterhielt).[5] This comment is found in a first listing of themes that keep on recurring and whose importance becomes evident precisely through their recurrence.

After a year she is eventually quite well again. The outcome is positive—an opening towards people: 'I longed for beings able to

---

2 Ibid., p. 358, 6f.

3 The theme of 'rebirth' is typical of the pietist movement. See Langen, *Wortschatz*, p. 149.

4 *Lehrjahre*, p. 358, 11ff.

5 Ibid., p. 358, 36ff.

return my love' (ich verlangte nach Wesen, die meine Liebe erwiderten).[6] This means, first of all, pets that her father supplies; but it mainly means the personal relationships that are characteristic of the rest of the chapter, concerning both people and God. Books that she now reads deepen her awareness of God's meaning for her:

> My longing after the Invisible, which I had always dimly felt, was strengthened by such means: for, in short, it was ordained that God should also be my confidant.

> Mein Hang zu dem Unsichtbaren, den ich immer auf eine dunkle Weise fühlte, ward dadurch nur vermehrt; denn ein für allemal sollte Gott auch mein Vertrauter sein.[7]

A further indication of the strength of her psyche (in contrast to the weakly fragility we might expect to result from a long period of illness) is found in her reference to dissection of poultry and pigs:

> To cut up a hen or a pig was quite a feast for me. I used to bring the entrails to my father, and he talked with me about them, as if I had been a student. With suppressed joy, he would often call me his son gone wrong.

> Ein Huhn, ein Ferkel aufzuschneiden, war für mich ein Fest. Dem Vater brachte ich die Eingeweide, und er redete mit mir darüber wie mit einem jungen Studenten und pflegte mich oft mit inniger Freude seinen missratenen Sohn zu nennen.[8]

She shows almost masculine interest in this occupation. If Emil Staiger finds here a certain indelicacy that is foreign to Goethe, it must at least be admitted that it is not the trait of a feeble psyche.[9] If there is any lack of balance here, it does not consist in a delicate feminine nature being made still more delicate through her sickness. Instead, her robustness in this instance continues the theme of her healthy tendency to take a live interest in things outside herself.[10]

By the time she is twelve years old, the aunt is orientated towards personal relationships, but on the religious level this still does not bring any particularly noteworthy effects. She reads several religious books, 'likes to hear about God' (hörte gern von Gott reden), and is proud that she can 'speak about Him better than my equals' (besser als meinesgleichen von ihm reden zu können).[11] But her religious instruc-

---

6 Ibid., p. 359, 17f.
7 Ibid., 39ff.
8 Ibid., p. 360, 30ff.
9 Staiger, *Goethe*, p. 141.
10 See above, beginning of chapter 6.
11 *Lehrjahre*, p. 361, 1f.

tion still does not preoccupy her any more than the other 'subjects' she is taking: French, dancing and drawing.

A further step in her development is made when she graduates from dancing with her sister to dancing with boys. The two most striking ones at the ball take notice precisely of her. During this brief episode she is still a child, but it contributes nevertheless 'to the forming of my heart' (zur Bildung meines Herzens).[12] Her involvement with the elder of the two represents her first experience of 'passion' (Leidenschaft), which preoccupied her like any other 'sickness' (Krankheit); the immediate effects, similar to those of the previous stage of her development, are, firstly: 'It made me calm, and drew me back from noisy pleasures' (dass sie mich still machte und mich von der schwärmenden Freude zurückzog).[13] This is a repetition of what we have already seen with regard to her sickness, circumstances influence her to withdraw from the exterior world for a time to help her focus on what she finds in her inner life. She is brought back to the source of her personal growth. This concentration of her inner life is a condition for what follows—that she finds God. There is a second effect closely linked with the first: 'I was alone, I was moved; and thoughts of God again occurred to me' (Ich war einsam und gerührt, und Gott fiel mir wieder ein).[14]

Here there seems to be a strengthening and deepening of her awareness of God:

> He was again my confidant, and I well remember with what tears I often prayed for this poor boy, who still remained sick.
>
> Er blieb mein Vertrauter, und ich weiss wohl, mit welchen Tränen ich für den Knaben, der fortkränkelte, zu beten anhielt.[15]

This small episode is rounded off with the comparison of the aunt's health with that of the two boys. It seems a clear indication from Goethe that so far the aunt has suffered no loss from her early sickness: a short time later the two boys die;[16] but she rapidly grows up, her health is perfect (ganz gesund)[17] and she begins to make her entry into the world.

---

12   Ibid., p. 362, 33.
13   Ibid., 27f.
14   Ibid., 28f.
15   Ibid., 29ff.
16   Ibid., 363, 29f.
17   Ibid.

7
Narziss

The stage is now set for the most striking part of the first main phase: the Narziss episode. As she grows older, the aunt is drawn more and more into a gay social life where she is surrounded by male attention. In referring to this period, it is not long before she starts to relate her activities to her religious experience. During all the hubbub around her,

> my feelings towards the Invisible One were almost totally extinguished. The hurry and the *crowd* I lived in distracted me and *carried* me *along* as in a *rapid stream*. These were the emptiest years of my life.

> (waren) die Empfindungen für den Unsichtbaren . . . bei mir fast ganz verloschen. Der *grosse Schwarm*, mit dem ich umgeben war, zerstreute mich und *riss* mich wie ein *starker Strom* mit *fort*. Es waren die leersten Jahre meines Lebens.[1]

Earlier references to the 'Invisible One' in the *Confession* were merely put side by side with other aspects of her experience. But here she contrasts the background experience of God with the foreground experience of the visible world, and it is evident that she now begins to see the latter as capable of interfering with the former aspect. The italicized words describe the foreground situation which threatens to preoccupy the aunt even to the extent of her losing sight of the other dimension of her experience. This period in which she lets herself be carried away by a torrent of material pleasures is the emptiest time she has known (die leersten Jahre meines Lebens).[2] The void, however, is later to be filled not by further pleasures of the same order but, in another dimension, by the 'Invisible One'. What is missing in her life is referred to indirectly

---

1 *Lehrjahre*, p. 364, 17ff.
2 Ibid.

where she says: 'I did not recollect myself, I never prayed, I never thought about myself or God (ich sammelte mich nicht, ich betete nicht, ich dachte nicht an mich noch an Gott).[3]

The aunt's evident awareness of a second, further dimension to experience brings us right to the central theme of our investigation. The object of her religious experience at this stage, i.e., her experience of the background dimension, is referred to in a definite and precise way: sometimes she speaks quite simply of 'God' (Gott), 'the Invisible One' (der Unsichbare Freund), 'my confidant' (mein Vertrauter), and the 'providential guidance' (Führung) that helps her avoid getting involved with any of the more distasteful male company around her.

It is at this stage that the aunt meets Narziss. Cultural interests they have in common are the basis of a friendship that is to deepen considerably when one day Narziss becomes the victim of physical violence. After a drunken and outraged companion has wounded Narziss both stand with daggers drawn. The aunt calmly leads Narziss away, while the men present hold his attacker. She calmly takes him into another room, bolts the door, and looks after his wounds, one of them a dangerous one in his head. Together with the presence of mind and psychological strength in the face of violence, there is also the lack of inhibition the aunt shows in her attention to Narziss: a short while later, she stands amongst a whole group of people, covered in the blood from Narziss' wounds and continues wetting his lips with wine while the doctor does the bandaging.[4] Although she feels the shock of the experience later, her whole response to the situation is quite normal and suggests strength rather than fragility. The strength and presence of mind she shows in this part of the story are qualities which form part of her basic character. There is nothing in the text to suggest that at this stage they derive from her religious experience; however, as the Narziss episode develops, we shall see that these qualities develop hand in hand with the deepening and strengthening of her religious commitment.

Seeing Narziss in such danger of losing his life brings the aunt's incipient love for him to light:

> The passion which was sleeping deep down in my heart had suddenly broken loose, like a flame getting air.

> der Affekt, der im tiefsten Grunde des Herzens ruhte, war auf einmal losgebrochen wie eine Flamme, welche Luft bekömmt.[5]

Now, what 'had formerly been "trifling and familiarity" has now grown

---

3   Ibid., 30f.

4   Linking the themes 'blood' and 'love' is common in pietist literature.

5   *Lehrjahre*, p. 369, 5ff.

into seriousness and inclination' (was vorher Tändelei und Gewohnheit
gewesen war, ward nun Ernst und Neigung).[6] This new situation has
two effects we need to note: firstly, 'the state of unrest in which I lived'
(die Unruhe, in der ich lebte);[7] and secondly,

> By such incessant agitations, I was once more led to recollect
> myself. The gaudy imagery of a distracted life, which used to
> hover day and night before my eyes, was at once blown away.

> Durch diese heftigen Erschütterungen ward ich wieder an mich
> selbst erinnert. Die bunten Bilder eines zerstreuten Lebens, die mir
> sonst Tag und Nacht vor Augen schwebten, waren auf einmal
> weggeblasen.[8]

The 'state of unrest' (Unruhe) she mentions and her penetration through
the surface existence she has been experiencing, mean for her a redis-
covery of herself (an mich selbst erinnert). This brings with it a new
awareness of God's presence in her life (and will provide the basis of a
further conflict between the two dimensions of her experience—in a
much more radical form than previously):

> My soul again began to awaken: but the greatly interrupted inti-
> macy with my Invisible Friend was not so easy to renew. We still
> continued at a certain distance: it was again something: but little
> by comparison with times of old.

> Meine Seele fing wieder an, sich zu regen; allein die sehr unter-
> brochene Bekanntschaft mit dem unsichtbaren Freunde war so
> leicht nicht wieder hergestellt. Wir blieben noch immer in ziem-
> licher Entfernung; es war wieder etwas, aber gegen sonst ein
> grosser Unterschied.[9]

It is interesting to see how direct the connection is for her between the
'awakening' (Regung) within her 'soul' (Seele) and the 'intimacy with
the Invisible Friend' (Bekanntschaft mit dem unsichtbaren Freunde).
The 'awakening' (Regung), which stems from her involvement with
Narziss, wakens her again to the presence of the 'Invisible Friend'
(Unsichtbaren Freund). This interconnection between the two spheres
is an essential aspect of the transcendence phenomenon as we see it in
the novel. The foreground aspect does not need to be annihilated or
left behind. Transcendence occurs in involvement in the foreground.
  Looking back on the period of 'unrest' (Unruhe) which follows what

---

6   Ibid., p. 370, 9f.
7   Ibid.
8   Ibid., 16ff.
9   Ibid., 19ff.

she calls 'four wild years' (vier wilde Jahre), she sees her attitude towards God not as one of total estrangement—she 'now begins to think of Him occasionally' (nun dachte ich dann und wann wieder an ihn)—but rather as one largely of indifference accompanied by a certain self-satisfaction:

> If God should please to think of me, all right. If not, I considered I had done my duty.

> wollte sich Gott mein Andenken gefallen lassen, so war es gut, wo nicht, so glaubte ich doch meine Schuldigkeit getan zu haben.[10]

But, as we shall see, this attitude is to be changed by future events: 'But, to change and purify my feelings, preparations were already made' (Meine Gesinnungen zu ändern und zu reinigen, waren aber auch schon Anstalten gemacht).[11]

The crisis

The remainder of the Narziss episode is relevant for the elements involved in the aunt's decision to break with him. There are serious weaknesses in his make-up which she is already aware of. Even his name, Narziss, was a joke that she has shared in. And now, when he speaks openly with her about marriage, she is aware that 'he was not a man one could deal with altogether openly' (dass er der Mann nicht war, mit dem man ganz gerade handeln konnte).[12] This latter comment is important as a sign of her independent, accurate judgment (again, a sign of health). The real problems begin for her once they are engaged. At first her relationship to him is a happy one, though only 'for a while' (auf kurze Zeit). We are justified in referring to this happiness as something depending almost entirely on her foreground experience, for in speaking of being 'truly happy' (wahrhaft glücklich) she qualifies it with the phrase: 'as one can be in the world' (wie man es in der Welt sein kann).[13] This is not to be understood merely to mean: 'as long as one lives' for the phrase 'truly happy' (wahrhaft glücklich) would not be an exaggerated description of her constant state resulting later from her religious experience when she was very much alive! Instead, the totality of her experience would show it to mean: 'so long as one seeks one's happiness primarily in the foreground of experience and misses the importance of the background aspect'; or, in other words: so long as one experiences life only in one dimension and not in the second dimension as well.

10   Ibid., p. 371, 14ff.
11   Ibid.
12   Ibid., p. 371, 31f.
13   Ibid., p. 372, 32.

Her brief happiness 'in the world' (in der Welt) is here accounted for by her total focussing on Narziss: 'he daily became more dear to me, my *whole soul* was his' (er ward mir immer lieber, meine ganze Seele hing an ihm).[14] But this foreground focussing is now accompanied simultaneously by a second background dimension:

> *Earthly* love itself concentrated my soul, and put its powers in motion; nor did it contradict my *intercourse with God.*

> Die *irdische* Liebe selbst konzentrierte meinen Geist und setzte ihn in Bewegung, und meine *Beschäftigung mit Gott* widersprach ihr nicht.[15]

The language used here (italicized words) points to two distinguishable aspects of her experience. She experiences the background aspect as a personal relationship to God.

It is worth noting in passing that the text contains further indications that her foreground preoccupation with Narziss is a total and radical one:

> Apart from Narziss, the whole world was dead for me; excepting him, there was nothing in it that had any charm. Even my love for dress was but the wish to please him.

> Die ganze Welt war mir ausser Narzissen tot, nichts hatte ausser ihm Reiz für mich. Selbst meine Liebe zum Putz hatte nur den Zweck, ihm zu gefallen.[16]

But, above all, the conflict between the two coexisting dimensions of her experience deserves our attention here. It raises the question of the relationship between the two dimensions. Purely theoretically, a lot could be said about this. But our task will be limited to examining what the text itself reveals to us about the relationship.

The first signs of a conflict between the two aspects appear when the aunt discovers that she and Narziss have quite different ideas about what is permitted them during the time of their engagement. It disturbs her to find that Narziss wants more freedom than she would allow and that, despite his praise of her attitude, he nevertheless tries to win her round. Her difficulty with him is not an isolated foreground experience; she sees it also in the second dimension: she finds it natural to turn to God with her problem:

> With God I had again become a little more acquainted. . . . I naturally complained to Him of what alarmed me.

---

14   Ibid., 35.

15   Ibid., p. 373, 14ff.

16   Ibid., 27ff.

Mit Gott war ich wieder ein wenig bekannter geworden. . . . Ganz
natürlich klagte ich ihm, was mich bange machte.[17]

At the time, she herself does not realize that she is caught up in the foreground situation to the extent of being no longer free. Although she
complains to God about what disturbs her, she does not realize till much
later 'that I myself was wishing and desiring it' (dass ich selbst das, was
mich bange machte, wünschte und begehrte).[18] Since she is no longer
free in the foreground aspect of her experience, but is attracted and
drawn in a way that she later recognizes as temptation,[19] and since at
the same time her attraction to God is becoming stronger, she finds herself in a conflict-situation. Examination of the text will show that her
situation is not simply reducible to a choice between foreground and
background.

If one can speak of the aunt's eventual renunciation of Narziss, this
cannot be taken in a sentimental sense. Her preference for the background element over the foreground, when the two are in conflict, is not
dictated by a sentimental withdrawal from a world she is incapable of
facing. Her attitude is not evasive. What she unsuccessfully strives to
achieve is the reconciliation of the two planes of experience. She is not
convinced that the two planes are in themselves irreconcilable. Quite
apart from the question of sentimentality, the aunt does not act according to the conviction that religion and involvement in the foreground
world are mutually exclusive. Her whole tendency, as shown in the text,
is to find a way of reconciling the two planes; and when, in the context
of her love for Narziss, this is found to be impossible, the reason for it
lies not in the incompatibility of the two planes themselves but in the
deviousness that forms part of Narziss' character: his lack of openness,
his pretence of respecting the aunt's convictions when his actions show
that he does not—these make it impossible for a deep relationship
between them to flourish. The radically defective orientation of Narziss
in his personal relationship to the aunt (not in his ethical convictions)
accounts for the impossibility of her reconciling the two planes. To
maintain the 'purity of existence' (Reinlichkeit des Daseins) which her
religious experience demands of her, she must give up her relationship
to Narziss.

But in this earlier stage when she is still involved in the conflict
between the two planes, there is an additional reason why she must re-
nounce Narziss: her own involvement with him is not free. She has
become entangled in this foreground relationship in such a way that

17 Ibid., 12, 15f.
18 Ibid., 18f.
19 Ibid.

her relationship to the 'Invisible Friend' is obscured. As long as the background relationship does not enjoy absolute primacy with her, a free involvement in the foreground is impossible and will always be open to question. A condition of possibility of radical, total, lasting commitment in the foreground is absolute background commitment. Once the primacy of the background is basically established in a person's life the person becomes free for the foreground. Then at least the subject is totally ready for foreground involvement (though still dependent on the disposition of other people and on outward circumstances). Though the foreground, through this basic liberation of the person, will be seen and appreciated in a much fuller way—seen according to its real value, seen for what it is—it will always be considered secondary in relation to the background, just as the creature, radically dependent in its being on the creator, will necessarily be seen as secondary to the creator. This secondariness is the truth about the created foreground world, just as primacy is the truth about the background world of the creator.

This interpretation of the relationship between the two planes—background and foreground—seems much nearer to a genuine appreciation of the aunt's inner attitude than the popular one expressed in the whisperings (at the end of the Narziss episode) about the 'woman who had valued God above her bridegroom' (die Gott mehr schätzte als ihren Bräutigam).[20] What becomes clear during the course of this episode is that the foreground may assert itself in her life, but only in so far as it harmonizes with her background experience. The awareness of harmony (with the background experience) becomes the criterion for making concrete foreground choices. This state of things is referred to (and admired) by Wilhelm where he later says to Natalie about her aunt:

> What most impressed me in this paper was, if I may term it so, the purity of existence not only of the writer herself, but of all that surrounded her; the independence of nature, the impossibility of admitting anything into her soul which would not harmonize with its own noble, loving tone.

> Was mir am meisten aus dieser Schrift entgegenleuchtete, war, ich möchte so sagen, die Reinlichkeit des Daseins, nicht allein ihrer selbst, sondern auch alles dessen, was sie umgab, diese Selbständigkeit ihrer Natur und die Unmöglichkeit, etwas in sich aufzunehmen, was mit der edlen, liebevollen Stimmung nicht harmonisch war.[21]

For the background aspect to be able to serve as a criterion for choices

---

20 Ibid., 383, 19f.
21 Ibid., p. 518, 9ff.

and decisions about foreground experience, it must have a constant, recognizable quality. One of its characteristics is given where the aunt says:

> He did not drive me back. On the smallest movement towards him, he left a gentle impression in my soul; and this impression caused me always to return.

> Er stiess mich nicht weg, auf die geringste Bewegung zu ihm hinterliess er einen sanften Eindruck in meiner Seele, und dieser Eindruck bewegte mich, ihn immer wieder aufzusuchen.[22]

It is clear that the 'gentle impression' was a repeated experience; precisely this drew her to seek God's presence, to live more and more in awareness of this background dimension. The experience is described in terms of her movement, her active seeking of the personal God. She speaks in a later passage about the 'direction' (Richtung) of her soul towards God.[23] Any foreground experience that puts an obstacle in the way of this movement towards God is, for her, as we shall see, out of harmony with her real self and therefore to be put aside. We shall come back to this point shortly.

Her awareness of the background aspect of experience is so alive, and her conviction that the personal God is the object of this aspect of her experience is so evident, that we may easily be led to think that God is for her just like another object of foreground experience. Narziss and God would be, in this case, rivals on the same foreground level. But in a passage which occurs shortly before the conflict between levels becomes fully evident, the aunt makes it clear that the question of compatibility is not posed inside the foreground area of experience, but rather concerns two different orders, one of which is subordinate to the other. That the two are not meant to be co-ordinate is indicated where, after mentioning her feelings for Narziss and her growing facility to speak to God about them, she says:

> Then feelings of another sort developed, but these did not contradict the former feelings. . . . They did not contradict each other, yet they were infinitely different.

> Da entwickelten sich Empfindungen anderer Art in meiner Seele, die jenen nicht widersprachen. . . . Sie widersprachen sich nicht und waren doch unendlich verschieden.[24]

After stressing how totally different the two kinds of feeling are, she goes on to distinguish them more precisely:

---

22 Ibid., p. 373, 23ff.

23 Ibid., p. 377, 6.

24 Ibid., p. 374, 13ff.

Narziss was the only image which hovered in my mind, and to which all my love was directed; but the other feeling was *not* directed towards any form, and yet it was unspeakably pleasing.

Narziss war das einzige Bild, das mir vorschwebte, auf das sich meine ganze Liebe bezog; aber das andere Gefühl bezog sich auf kein Bild und war unaussprechlich angenehm.[25]

We see here that:

1 there is total focussing on the foreground;
2 the background dimension is referred to explicitly and directly;
3 the aunt says quite definitely that no image is involved in the background aspect of her experience. Here she finds herself confronted with 'something' that does not present a positive, representable content to her consciousness. It is thus made quite clear that the object of her experience has two distinguishable aspects, permitting us to speak of a foreground-background structure. The significance of this structure in her experience will become increasingly evident.

Conclusion of the Narziss episode

A year after the beginning of her friendship with Narziss comes the climax. After living for months in high hope of obtaining a favourable post, Narziss is to be passed over for another, inferior candidate. The whole question of Narziss' advancement is vital for the aunt, because on it depends the question of whether they could marry or not. As the time comes for deciding whether Narziss or another should get the post in question, he and his friends exert all possible influence. As for the aunt's own attitude in this moment 'when my whole destiny was to be decided' (in dem sich mein ganzes Schicksal entscheiden sollte), we read:

While Narziss and all our friends were making every effort to efface some impressions which obstructed him at Court, . . . I turned with my request to my Invisible Friend.

Indess Narziss und alle Freunde sich bei Hofe die möglichste Mühe gaben, gewisse Eindrücke, die ihm ungünstig waren, zu vertilgen . . . wendete ich mich mit meinem Anliegen zu dem unsichtbaren Freunde.[26]

We see here again a twofold dimension: the preoccupation, this time, of

---

25 Ibid.
26 Ibid., p. 376., 9ff.

the others with the foreground, concrete affairs, and the aunt's turning
to the background, to the 'Invisible Friend' (dem unsichtbaren Freunde).
On the strength of this latter relationship she is able to face the concrete
situation (which concerns her as much as any, and more than most!)
with far greater freedom than the others. She has a grip on the total
situation: her basic happiness is secured by the background relationship; despite the fact that she sees Narziss' struggle as her own cause,
she remains free enough and rests sufficiently in the friendship with
the 'Invisible Friend' not to need to try and sway the decision one way
or another by her prayer. What she wishes is clear: that Narziss get the
position, but, as she says:

> My prayer was not importunate; and I did not require that it
> should happen for the sake of my petition.

> Meine Bitte war nicht ungestüm, und ich forderte nicht, dass es
> um meines Gebets willen geschehen sollte.[27]

Despite her real foreground involvement, she is able to retain an inner
freedom based on her continual moving in the background dimension
where she is 'received so kindly, that I gladly came again' (so freundlich
aufgenommen, dass ich gern wiederkam).[28] This kind of liberty can
easily be interpreted as a cool attitude that is foreign to real love: if the
aunt really loved Narziss, she would not be content to await the outcome
of the decision that is vital for their marriage. But the supposition in
this kind of argument is gratuitous: namely, that the background and
foreground spheres of experience are so radically different from one
another that they are hardly mutually relevant at all—as if religion were
one thing and the sphere of personal, social relationships were another.
The 'schöne Seele' insists that she does love Narziss, and it is the critic's
role to reconcile this love with her love for the 'Invisible Friend', unless
the author shows in the novel that her statements are not to be taken
seriously.

We have already dealt above with the relationship between the foreground and the background spheres of experience when a conflict arises
between them.[29] There we could consider the aunt's freedom mainly by
analysis of its negation, i.e., her unfree involvement with Narziss. But
here we have an example of the positive side of it. Her relationship to
the 'Invisible Friend' has become primary in fact. Although her total
fulfilment depends also on her foreground relationships, her basic fulfilment is realized to the extent that the 'Invisible Friend' enjoys

27   Ibid., 16.
28   Ibid., 13.
29   See pp. 51ff.

primacy in her life. Basic fulfilment consisting, on the one hand, in the discovery and acceptance of oneself as radically dependent on the background and, on the other hand, in the discovery and acceptance of this latter as the foundation of one's own being, gives the person a strong enough hold on meaning to enable him to become free with regard to the foreground. If full acceptance of his own dependence on the background does not disturb us, neither should his full acceptance of the dependence of others on the background present problems to us. In the aunt's conviction, nothing in the foreground world can lay an absolute claim on us and we cannot lay an absolute claim on anything in the foreground world—provided we want to keep open our basic relationship to the background world. This gives the basis for distance from everyone and everything in the foreground. Distance is the only correct attitude until it is clear what concrete relationship is desirable and possible; and even when the relationship is solidified the same structure remains: the solidification of a relationship of the person with the foreground does not destroy his total dependence on the background. Thus he will always need to remain free in his foreground commitment.

The account of the aunt's reaction to the news of Narziss' defeat throws further light on her total attitude. Her real involvement in the situation is put beyond doubt when we read:

> I was dreadfully troubled at this news; I hastened to my room, the door of which I locked behind me. The first fit of grief went off in a flood of tears.

> Ich erschrak heftig über die Zeitung und eilte in mein Zimmer, das ich fest hinter mir zumachte. Der erste Schmerz löste sich in Tränen auf.[30]

This reflects the foreground aspect of her involvement. The other aspect however is immediately felt: 'The next thought was: yet it was not by chance that it happened' (der nächste Gedanke war: Es ist aber doch nicht von ungefähr geschehen).[31] Just as she has been free to leave the decision to the 'Invisible Friend' she is now with equal freedom able to accept the decision. With the return of this background aspect into her conscious experience, she experiences the typical accompanying feelings:

> The gentlest emotions then pressed in upon me, and dispelled all the clouds of sorrow. I felt that, with help like this, there was nothing one might not endure. At dinner I was quite cheerful, to the great astonishment of all the house.

---

30   *Lehrjahre,* p. 376, 19ff.
31   Ibid., 21f.

Nun drangen die sanftesten Empfindungen, die alle Wolken des Kummers zerteilten, herbei; ich fühlte, dass sich mit dieser Hülfe alles ausstehn liess. Ich ging heiter zu Tische, zum Erstaunen meiner Hausgenossen.[32]

This inner experience, characterized by gentleness, tranquility (being rid of 'clouds of sorrow' [Wolken des Kummers]), strength ('endure' [ausstehn]) and cheerfulness puts the aunt in a position to strengthen and console Narziss: 'Narziss had less strength than I, and I had to comfort him' (Narziss hatte weniger Kraft als ich, und ich musste ihn trösten).[33] It is precisely her inner experience that carries her through the crisis:

All this I felt deeply on his account and mine; all this too I ultimately carried to the place where my petitions had already been so well received.

alles fühlte ich tief um seinet- und meinetwillen, und alles trug ich zuletzt an den Ort, wo mein Anliegen so wohl aufgenommen wurde.[34]

Though Narziss' failure is to have a decisive influence on their relationship, no clear decision is reached for almost another year. Watching the aunt bring the whole Narziss episode to a conclusion will help us understand with more precision the characteristics of her experience, and especially the influence the background relationship exerts on her concrete living. The accent will be on her decision-making. It will become apparent above all that the more intense her background experience becomes the more she is capable of thinking and deciding for herself.
    When we read:

The *gentler* these experiences were, the more often I endeavoured to renew them; I hoped continually to meet with *comfort* where I had so often met with it; but I was as one that goes to warm himself in the *sunshine,* while there is something standing in the way that makes a shadow

Je *sanfter* diese Erfahrungen waren, desto öfter suchte ich sie zu erneuern und den *Trost* immer da, wo ich ihn zo oft gefunden hatte; allein ich fand ihn nicht immer, es wahr mir wie einem, der sich *an der Sonne* wärmen will, und dem etwas im Wege steht, das Schatten macht[35]

---

32 Ibid., 25ff.
33 Ibid., 30.
34 Ibid., 35ff.
35 Ibid., 38ff.

we find the aunt trying to keep this background experience alive. The italicized words indicate how she characterizes it. The description squares with what we have just seen as the strengthening experience that carries her through the immediate crisis. The continuation of the passage just quoted shows that the same experience serves as a criterion for right practical judgment. In her determination to keep the background (seen as primary and constant in comparison with the secondary and changing foreground) experience intact, she must ask herself what is, in her present situation, obstructing her contact with the 'sunshine' (Sonne) and casting shadows. She discovers that it all depends on her own inner attitude:

> If this (the soul) was not turned in the straightest direction towards God, I still continued cold.

> wenn die (die Seele) nicht ganz in der geradesten Richtung zu Gott gekehrt war, so blieb ich kalt.[36]

Finding an answer to the question: 'What hinders this direction?' (Was verhindert diese Richtung?) would make clear to her what practical judgment is required. She enjoys the advantage of possessing a clear criterion which is not just some abstract rational principle, but an inner, constant, personally experienced relationship to the 'Invisible Friend', whose reciprocation and answer she is aware of as long as she retains her inner freedom in her foreground relationships.

It takes her almost a year to realize fully that precisely the lack of freedom in her foreground involvement is blocking her background relationship. The required honesty with herself does not come all at once:

> For it was not long till I had got on the right track; but I would not confess it, and I sought a thousand escapes.

> denn ich kam bald auf die Spur; aber ich wollte es nicht gestehen und suchte tausend Ausflüchte.[37]

Although she very soon sees that 'the straight direction of my soul' (die gerade Richtung meiner Seele) is being disturbed by 'foolish dissipations, and preoccupation with unworthy things' (törichte Zerstreuung und Beschäftigung mit unwürdigen Sachen)[38]—this is the shadow in question—she is not able to free herself, because pushing these things aside would affect Narziss too. He is afraid they would be laughed at and considered overscrupulous if they retired from what, in the aunt's

36   Ibid., p. 377, 6f.
37   Ibid., 12ff.
38   Ibid., 17ff.

experience, is a frivolous and foolish round of social activities. In her endeavour not to hurt Narziss, she compromises herself:

> My inmost feelings contradicted me too often . . . I was hemmed in as by a ring drawn round me; . . . I required some strong support; and God would not grant it me, while I was running around with the cap and bells.

> Mein Inneres widersprach mir zu oft . . . Ich war nun einmal in einen Kreis hineingesperrt; . . . ich bedurfte einer kräftigen Unterstützung, und die verlieh mir Gott nicht, wenn ich mit der Schellenkappe herumlief.[39]

The last line quoted focusses our attention on the centre of the aunt's own particular problem: 'the cap and bells' (Schellenkappe) do not fit her. She does not find such things bad in themselves. Her difficulty consists in her own lack of freedom when she gets involved in this sphere:

> For no sooner had I clothed myself in the garment of folly than it came to be something more than a mask; the foolishness pierced and penetrated me through and through.

> Denn sobald ich mich in das Gewand der Torheit kleidete, blieb es nicht bloss bei der Maske, sondern die Narrheit durchdrang mich sogleich durch und durch.[40]

She is not speaking of this sphere as one who tries to arrive at a judgment about its moral worth. She does not speak of it in general terms, but rather of its direct effect on her. For her personally it is not the right thing, because 'those occupations distracted my attention and disturbed my peace of mind' (jene Handlungen, die mich nun einmal zerstreuten und meinen innern Frieden störten).[41] She wants to regulate her involvement with them in such a way 'that my heart . . . might still be open to the influences of the Invisible Being' (dass dabei mein Herz für die Einwirkungen des unsichtbaren Wesens offen bliebe).[42] Her attitude is neither consciously nor unconsciously prudish. She reflects directly on the problem

> that in my twenty-second year, and even earlier, I lost all relish for the recreations with which people of that age are harmlessly delighted.

---

39 Ibid., 23ff.
40 Ibid., p. 378, 13ff.
41 Ibid., 8.
42 Ibid., 10.

dass ich im zweiundzwanzigsten Jahre, ja fruher, kein Vergnügen an Dingen fand, die Leute von diesem Alter unschuldig belustigen können.[43]

The last three words quoted give her positive attitude to the kind of 'recreation' (Vergnügen) in question. Then she has to ask herself: if this is all right for others of my age, why do I experience it as wrong for me? The answer is one based, not on abstract considerations, but on a most personal, concrete aspect of her inner experience:

I knew from experiences which had reached me unsought, that there are loftier emotions which afford us a contentment such as it is vain to seek in amusements.

Ich wusste aus Erfahrungen, die ich ungesucht erlangt hatte, dass es höhere Empfindungen gebe, die uns ein Vergnügen wahrhaftig gewährten, das man vergebens bei Lustbarkeiten sucht.[44]

This awareness of a pleasure (Vergnügen) that is more substantial because belonging to a higher order does not in principle cause a conflict with the other kind of pleasure referred to. For the aunt, however, the conflict is in fact there:

However much a man might hanker after wine, all desire of drinking would forsake him, if he should be placed among barrels in a cellar, where the foul air was likely to suffocate him. Pure air is more than wine.

Wer den Wein noch so sehr liebt, dem wird alle Lust zum Trinken vergehen, wenn er sich bei vollen Fässern in einem Keller befände, in welchem die verdorbene Luft ihn zu ersticken drohte. Reine Luft ist mehr als Wein . . .[45]

That there is a conflict is apparent. Where does the cause of it lie? The comparison points to the fact that it lies not in the 'wine'. This is seen as both positive and good. The cause of the conflict is to be found in the aunt's own lack of freedom. Her attitude is anything but a shying away from a sphere of experience found unpleasant, for example, for lack of success. There is nothing to suggest that she is inferior in this sphere. Nor has she any lack of attraction to it. She herself says:

But social pleasures and youthful distractions must have had a powerful charm for me.

---

43 Ibid., 19ff.
44 Ibid., 25ff.
45 Ibid., p. 379, 4ff.

Aber die geselligen Vergnügungen und Zerstreuungen der Jugend
mussten doch notwendig einen starken Reiz für mich haben.[46]

And a little later she speaks of 'something within me that longed for
earthly pleasures' (etwas in mir, . . . das sich nach den sinnlichen
Freuden hinsehnte).

The difficulty for her—and the precise cause of her conflict—is that:
'it was not possible for me to engage in them as if not engaged in them'
(es [war] mir nicht möglich . . . sie zu tun, als täte ich sie nicht).[47]

This means that in her involvement with this particular aspect of her
environment, she is unable to keep herself inwardly free. She lacks the
balance that would enable her to keep this foreground aspect in its
proper perspective, which in practice would mean keeping herself open,
during her foreground involvement, for 'higher joys'. When she says it
had not been possible for her 'to be engaged in them as if not engaged
in them' (sie zu tun, als täte ich sie nicht), she is alluding to the scriptural
text where St Paul writes: 'And those who have to deal with the world
should not become engrossed in it.'[48] Earlier verses of the text show that
this is not to be understood as an opting out of involvement with people;
the passage is rather concerned with the fact that the span of human life
is limited and that the Christian has to keep the temporal, limited aspects
of his concrete experience in proper perspective. (When Paul writes:
'Those who have wives should live as though they had none . . .' it would
be a serious misinterpretation to think that he meant to introduce a celi-
bate frame of mind [or way of acting] into married life. Whatever may
be said about Paul's own strong preference for celibacy, the free choice
between marriage [seen in its full, vibrant reality] and celibacy remains.
The dignity of marriage itself in St Paul's eyes is seen in the comparison
he makes between the union of the husband and wife on the one hand
and the union between Christ and the Church [His Body] on the other.[49]
Paul's intention in saying 'as if they had none' is not to rob marriage of
its concrete significance, but to underline the need for maintaining one's
inner freedom within the framework of the full, resonant marital commitment. The next verse [30] about weeping and rejoicing as though
one did not, offers support to the proposed interpretation. The letters of
St Paul give ample evidence that he wept and rejoiced abundantly in his
sincere involvement. Yet he also kept his inner freedom.)

Though the aunt has previously been unfree, because social pleasures

46   Ibid., p. 378, 31ff.
47   Ibid.
48   1 Corinthians 7, 31.
49   Ephesians 5, 25-30.

'. . . then dazzled and confused me and even threatened to gain the mastery over me' (mich damals irremachte, ja Meister über mich zu werden drohte),[50] she emphasizes that this situation belongs to the past. She could do the same things now (at the time of writing) even 'with entire coldness' (mit grosser Kälte).[51] Her control has grown in the meantime. The fact that she could later have done the same things without losing her inner freedom points to the fact that in her whole conflict everything centres around this point of her freedom and not around the moral value of the things themselves.

The rest of the Narziss episode is the story of her struggle to get free from entanglements. This means first of all, in practice, taking a firm stand with Narziss himself and not letting him keep her imprisoned in a world where she can not be free. It means, secondly, facing a lot of criticism which is most unpleasant. On the way to attaining a greater inner freedom, she has also to become free in regard to outside influences.

She resolves the immediate conflict by taking the steps necessary to free herself for the friendship with the 'Invisible Friend'. In watching the steps she takes, we can observe the relevance the background relationship has for her concrete living.

> I acted immediately. I drew off the mask, and on all occasions did as my heart directed.

> Gedacht, gewagt. Ich zog die Maske ab und handelte jedesmal, wie mir's ums Herz war.[52]

This means that she now begins to follow her own judgment without wondering too much about Narziss' opinions. Narziss begins to withdraw from her and, the further he withdraws, the freer she becomes. Now comes a series of difficulties stemming from her family: 'They questioned me, they showed surprise' (Man befragte mich, man wollte sich verwundern).[53] Her replies are firm and decisive, full of spirit and independence, expressing her deep attachment to Narziss, but also stressing her need for freedom to live according to her convictions. One passage in particular is worth quoting, to dispel any thought that the aunt is a wilting violet:

---

50 *Lehrjahre*, p. 378, 31ff.

51 Ibid.

52 Ibid., p. 379, 20.

53 Ibid., 29.

I explained to them with stout defiance, that up to now I had
made abundant sacrifices: that I was ready to share still further
and even till the end of my life all the hardships that befall him;
but that I required full freedom in my conduct, that what I did
and left undone must depend upon my own conviction; that I
would never stubbornly cling to my own opinion, and was willing
to be reasoned with; yet, as it concerned my own happiness, the
decision must be my own, and I would tolerate no kind of con-
straint.

Ich erklärte mit männlichem Trotz, dass ich mich bisher genug
aufgeopfert habe, dass ich bereit sei, noch ferner bis ans Ende
meines Lebens alle Widerwärtigkeiten mit ihm zu teilen; dass ich
aber für meine Handlungen völlige Freiheit verlange, dass mein
Tun und Lassen von meiner Überzeugung abhängen müsse; dass
ich zwar niemals eigensinnig auf meiner Meinung beharren, viel-
mehr jede Gründe gerne anhören wolle, aber da es mein eignes
Glück betreffe, müsse die Entscheidung von mir abhängen, und
keine Art von Zwang würde ich dulden.[54]

She is so sure of her position that she can even enjoy the debates. Her
vigorous attitude is further indicated in expressions like: 'I yielded
not a hair's breadth' (ich wich nicht ein Haar breit), 'sent packing'
(derb abgefertigt), 'I soon conquered' (siegte ich bald); and in referring to a pestering aunt of hers: 'that she had no say in the matter in
any way' (dass sie in keinem Sinne eine Stimme in dieser Sache
habe).[55] In the discussion with her father there is a change of key. Tied
up by his logic, she no longer acts with 'stout defiance' (männlichem
Trotz), but appeals to his heart: 'I came out with the most pathetic
pleadings. I gave free course to my tongue and to my tears' ([ich]
brach . . . in die affektvollsten Vorstellungen aus. Ich liess meiner
Zunge und meinen Tränen freien Lauf).[56] The passage that follows
shows that she is prepared to sacrifice everything to live according to
her convictions. There is no doubting either her femininity or her
backbone.

A final word is needed a propos of her definitive break with Narziss.
Her new attitude has served to make him withdraw though he does not
try to clarify their relationship. Not satisfied to be left dangling, the
aunt waits till she is in the frame of mind that is becoming characteristic of her: 'calm' (still), 'strong' (stark), 'peaceful' (ruhig) and
'secure' (gesetzt);[57] and then she writes him a polite note asking why

54 Ibid., 30ff.
55 Ibid., p. 380, 12ff.
56 Ibid.
57 Ibid., p. 381, 29f.

he no longer visits her. His answer avoids the central issue. He obviously does not have the courage to break off the engagement. The aunt herself breaks it off and declares to her relations and friends that: 'the affair was altogether settled' (die Sache sei abgetan). When she later hears that Narziss is to marry someone else, the Narziss episode is completely finished: 'my own tranquility was quite complete' (Meine Beruhigung [war] ganz vollkommen).[58] We leave the episode on a positive note:

With good health, I enjoyed an indescribable composure of mind. . . . Young and full of sensibility, I thought the universe a thousand times more beautiful than formerly. . . . And now as I did not conceal my piety, I likewise had the courage to admit my love for the sciences and arts. I drew, painted, read; and found enough people to support me; . . . I was attracted to social life. . . . Before long my acquaintances were very numerous; not at home only, but likewise among people further away.

Ich genoss bei einer guten Gesundheit eine unbeschreibliche Gemütsruhe . . . Jung und voll Empfindung, wie ich war, deuchte mir die Schöpfung tausendmal schöner als vorher . . . Da ich mich einmal meiner Frömmigkeit nicht schämte, so hatte ich Herz, meine Liebe zu Künsten und Wissenschaften nicht zu verbergen. Ich zeichnete, malte, las und fand Menschen genug, die mich unterstützten; . . . Ich hatte eine Neigung zum gesellschaftlichen Leben . . . Meine Bekanntschaften wurden erst recht weitläufig, nicht nur mit Einheimischen . . . sondern auch mit Fremden.[59]

The health, peace, confidence, activity, capacity for broad social contact—all these inwardly linked with her strength as based on her background relationship. She is convinced that: 'In these higher joys there is also a secret treasure for strengthening the spirit in misfortune' (dass in diesen höhern Freuden zugleich ein geheimer Schatz zur Stärkung im Unglück aufbewahrt sei).[60] Thus the significance of the background element in her experience is apparent: without this aspect the life, strength and autonomy she manifests in her decision-making would lack a foundation.

---

58 Ibid., p. 382, 29.
59 Ibid., 37ff.
60 Ibid., p. 378, 28ff.

8

The Authenticity of her Experience

Once the Narziss episode is closed, the aunt's experience begins to broaden out. The personal growth she has gone through means that her company is prized by many people outside her immediate family circle, including 'a large number of princes, counts, and lords of the Empire' (einen grossen Teil der Fürsten, Gräfen und Herren des Reichs).[1] Of special importance is the contact with the uncle, her father's step-brother, who represents for us the protector of the world in which Natalie grew up and into which Wilhelm is soon to be introduced.

When the uncle is called the step-brother of her father this is already a hint that her relationship with the uncle will not be harmonious. Various factors have contributed towards making the uncle 'unbending' (unbiegsam). (This is the aunt's judgment.)[2] Added to this was his incapacity, despite his highly cultivated intelligence, to come to grips with the aunt's kind of inner experience: 'for here the question was about emotions, of which he had not the slightest awareness' (denn hier war von Empfindungen die Rede, von denen er gar keine Ahnung hatte). It was clear to her that 'he had not the slightest notion of what formed the ground of all my conduct' (dass er von dem, worin der Grund aller meiner Handlungen lag, offenbar keinen Begriff hatte).[3] It becomes clear in the course of the novel that the uncle writes her off as some kind of religious eccentric. But she is in fact much more conscious that his judgment is implicitly negative than he is himself —as she shows with a light touch of irony:

---

1 *Lehrjahre*, p. 383, 32.
2 Ibid., p. 384, 18.
3 Ibid., p. 385, 1f.

His feelings towards me he likewise showed us pantomimically, by procuring me a post as Canoness, and frequently I could not help, in secret, smiling at the role, which now as Canoness, as a young and pious Canoness, I was playing in the world.

Seine Gesinnungen gegen mich gab er gleichfalls pantomimisch zu erkennen, indem er mir den Platz einer Stiftsdame verschaffte . . . und manchmal musste ich über die Person, die ich nun als Stiftsdame, als junge und fromme Stiftsdame, in der Welt spielte, heimlich lächeln.[4]

Goethe is smiling with her at the expense of the uncle, who is hardly aware of the humour of the situation. (See the humour of the repetition of the word 'Canoness' [Stiftsdame] in the passage just quoted, and also the reference to her 'gala livery' [Galalivree][5]—the garb she has to wear as Canoness.)

This new start is soon followed by further problems. Again her health, taxed by the new round of unaccustomed activities, gives her trouble:

I was attacked by a haemorrhage, which, although it did not prove dangerous or lasting, yet left a weakness after it, perceptible for many a day.

(Es) überfiel mich ein Blutsturz, der, ob er gleich nicht gefährlich war und schnell vorüberging, doch lange Zeit eine merkliche Schwachheit hinterliess.[6]

A further ordeal comes when her mother is stricken with the illness of which she dies five years later. In the meantime her father too becomes sick. These three illnesses represent for the aunt a period for testing the authenticity of her religious experience. It would be a mistake to concentrate onesidedly on the aunt's own sickness. Her trial is much more complex. Her own sickness, like that of her parents, is mentioned to show the growth that takes place in this next phase of her life. Of her own sickness we read that she remained 'joyful' (freudig) during it, that nothing 'bound me to the world' (nichts fesselte mich an die Welt), and that she is 'in the most cheerful and calm state' (in dem heitersten und ruhigsten Zustande).[7] These aspects of her inner experience remind us of the kind of strength she showed in the crisis

---

4   Ibid., 11ff, 34ff.
5   Ibid., p. 386, 3.
6   Ibid., 27ff.
7   Ibid., 31.

of the Narziss episode; and here again the test of her inner strength raises the question of the religious dimension of her experience:

> It was now that I could try whether the path which I had chosen was the path of fantasy or truth; whether I had merely thought as others showed me, or the object of my faith had a reality.

> Nun konnte ich mich prüfen, ob auf dem Wege, den ich eingeschlagen, Wahrheit oder Phantasie sei, ob ich vielleicht nur nach andern gedacht, oder ob der Gegenstand meines Glaubens eine Realität habe.[8]

Here the question of the authenticity is directly posed, and the purpose of the episode is to continue to present her experience as genuine and to show her becoming increasingly independent in her judgment as her religious experience deepens.

The result of the trial is: 'It gave my conviction great support that I always found the latter' (zu meiner grössten Unterstützung fand ich immer das letztere), namely that 'the object of my faith had a reality' (der Gegenstand meines Glaubens eine Realität habe).[9] She is continually able to fall back on her experience of the 'straight direction of my heart to God' (gerade Richtung meines Herzens zu Gott).[10] This and the fellowship of the 'beloved ones' is what 'made everything easy for me' (was mir alles erleichterte).[11] Her conviction of having a personal relationship to God (and to others, in the context of this religious experience) grows through the trials she is subjected to, and it becomes clearer, even for her, 'what the ground of all my conduct consists in' (worin der Grund aller meiner Handlungen lag),[12] namely God. This experience of God is implicitly described as one of coolness, freshness—she is like the traveller protected from the heat by a shadow. Similarly, she has the experience of being protected. God is the 'place of refuge' (Schutzort) for her when pressure from elsewhere becomes too strong.

The idea of God as a 'place of refuge' is not escapist. It reflects a typically pietist attitude towards God and has its roots in the Old and New Testament where God is seen as the protector of His people. Images that are very closely related to that of the 'place of refuge'[13] are those of God's wings giving protection. (See *Hide me in the shade of*

---

8   Ibid., p. 387, 13ff.
9   Ibid., 15f.
10 Ibid., 17f.
11 Ibid., 19.
12 Ibid., p. 385, 2.
13 Ibid., p. 387, 21.

your wings, Ps. 17, 8; *I shelter in the shade of your wings*, Ps. 57, 2; *I rejoice in the shade of your wings*, Ps. 63, 8; and also *How often have I longed to gather your children as a hen gathers her chicks under her wings*, Mt. 23, 37.) Images such as these are not meant to express a flight from the world, amounting to renunciation of it, but rather a sense of security in the world. The basis of such security is one's intensely personal relationship to God who is the protector. See St John's Gospel, where Jesus prays to the Father for His disciples:

> I am not asking you to remove them from the world but to protect them from the evil one. Jn. 17, 14.)

The authenticity of the aunt's experience is clearly to be seen in relation to some kind of objective reality. This does not mean that she feels the need to establish the existence of God by any objectifying process such as might enable her to defend and demonstrate the validity of her experience. Rather, she is satisfied to find her conviction that God is real verified for her by the fact that she feels herself protected and buoyed up by her confidence in God; one of the most concrete manifestations of God's reality for her is the peace and serenity she experiences when she turns towards Him for comfort. Her religious experience can be called authentic in so far as its basis in reality is proven at least to her satisfaction; it is also authentic in the sense that it is not divorced from real existence—i.e., her real existence—since it enables her to face the trials and shoulder the burdens which come into her life; a further sense in which her experience may be termed authentic is that it brings about the development of her true self. Acceptance of the background goes hand in hand with her radical self-acceptance as creature.

In a letter to Schiller (18 March 1795) Goethe refers to the *Confession* in a way that raises doubts about the validity or authenticity of the aunt's religious experience:

> The whole (of the sixth book) rests on the noblest illusions and the most delicate confusion of the subjective with the objective.

This must be taken in some way to refer to her convictions about the reality of her 'Invisible Friend'. But if her convictions are based on illusions and misconceptions, if what she thinks to be objective is really subjective, what is the value of her experience?

The first point we need to stress is that these words of Goethe are extraneous to the novel itself and therefore have very limited value for its interpretation. It is a commonplace of literary criticism that the author is not necessarily a helpful interpreter of his own work. As Emil Staiger says in his long essay on Goethe's *Faust I:*

We insist that the commentator can and should understand a work
(a poem, play, novel, etc.) better than the person who wrote it. . . .
He (the author) does not read his lines with the conscientiousness
and respect that we (the critics and commentators) owe them. . . .
He does not see his text from a philologist's point of view. . . .
With Goethe this is even more the case than with other writers,
for he does not treat poetry with anything like the 'liturgical'
solemnity that we find in Klopstock, Hölderlin, Stifter and
George.[14]

But even Goethe's own comment, damning as it may seem at first sight,
can be reconciled with the validity of the aunt's experience. Goethe himself mentions the confusion of the subjective with the objective. The fact
that he uses such categories implies that he finds that they correspond to
the real situation: that there is, for Goethe, something objective, enjoying at least relative independence of one's subjectivity; and, in fact,
Goethe's classicism finds ample room for an objective reality, a real
structure in things, and a divine sphere which impinges on human
experience. It is only when the question of interpreting this objective
divine sphere arises that Goethe becomes extremely sceptical—and this
is the scepticism which we find in the letter to Schiller: since the aunt,
like other pietists, so readily identifies a personal God and, more specifically, Christ with the divine sphere (the background), Goethe speaks
of her confusion of the subjective and objective and of her illusions.
When she speaks of the divine in personal and even Christian terms, she
is employing what she herself considers an authentic interpretation of
her religious experience. Goethe, in the passage quoted, does not admit
that it is an authentic interpretation.

But underlying the interpretation, present in the aunt's consciousness
—alongside and showing through the interpretation—there is the actual
experience (which she has interpreted in Christian terms). It is true that
the interpretation is not separable from the experience itself—the
experience itself will always include the interpretation as part of its
structure; but once the need for interpretation as part of the formal
structure of one's experience is recognized, the actual content of the
experience can be left aside and the experience itself focussed on. It is
the background-foreground structure of this experience and the energies
and life it supports (joy, strength, peace, harmony, autonomy, etc.)[15]
which interest us here and which we claim are authentic. If we relate
Goethe's negative comment to the interpretative aspect of the aunt's
total experience, it is easy to see that Goethe, unwilling to commit him-

14 Staiger, *Goethe*, p. 363.
15 See above, chapter 4.

self to any form of religion with dogmatic and historical claims, would look on her Christian interpretation as illusory; at the same time it is easy to see that he could accept a person's experience as authentic without adopting their interpretation of it.

As early as 1775, in his *Sturm und Drang* period, Goethe showed that he distinguished clearly between experience and interpretation. In *Urfaust*, Goethe's first attempt at *Faust*, Gretchen is questioning the hero about his religion. She is worried that he does not seem to esteem it highly, especially Christianity. Faust answers:

> Erfüll davon dein Herz, so gross es ist
> Und wenn du ganz in dem Gefühle selig bist
> Nenn es dann, wie du willst
> Nenn's Glück! Herz! Liebe! Gott!
> Ich habe keinen Namen
> Dafür. Gefühl ist alles,
> Name ist Schall und Rauch,
> Umnebelnd Himmelsglut.[16]

This reality that he is unwilling to name works 'invisibly-visibly near her'[17] (Gretchen) when Faust and she are together. From this it is evident that the reality is distinct from each of them, though it can fill them (see Erfüll, 1. 1143). Faust himself has no name for this reality. He sees the most divergent possibilities: happiness, heart, love, God. Interpreting such reality by naming it does not appeal to him. Name is 'sound' and 'smoke'. To have experienced the reality is the important thing (Gefühl ist alles). To try earnestly to name it is to surround its glow (Himmelsglut) with cloud.

That this attitude of Goethe's towards finding authentic interpretations of reality belonged not just to his early period but remained with him all his life can be seen from the way he treated Christianity as a kind of myth in his *Faust I* (classical period), in the final chapter of his novel, *Die Wahlverwandtschaften*—where Ottilie's holiness is crowned with miracle-working after her death—and in *Wilhelm Meisters Wanderjahre*, where the story of the Flight into Egypt is treated with a great deal of reverence. In none of these works could Goethe be said to accept Christianity as the authentic interpretation of experience. The figures in these 'myths' stand for or at least point to something real, though Goethe himself would not accord them the same historical and dogmatic importance claimed for them by orthodox Christians.

Thus we seem to have in Goethe's work itself the basis for distinguishing between interpretation and the experience being interpreted, and for

---

16   Goethe, *Faust I, Werke*, vol. 3, (Hamburger Ausgabe), 11. 3451-3458.
17   Ibid., 1. 3450.

supposing that Goethe was interested primarily, perhaps even exclusively, in the latter.

As if aware that her attitude is in danger of being falsely interpreted, the aunt takes pains to distinguish it from that of people who want to pounce on every insignificant occurrence and use it as a direct proof for the validity of their experience. She is cautious about making too much of 'isolated instances' (einzelne Fälle).[18] The individual instances, looked at in isolation, seem insignificant. But the consistency with which they occur makes of them a phenomenon that has to be accounted for. She writes: 'My soul . . . hastened to the place of refuge, . . . and never did it return empty' (meine Seele [eilte] nach diesem Schutzort . . . und kam niemals leer zurück).[19]

And again:

> I can say that I never returned empty, when under pressure and in need I called on God.

> Ich darf sagen, ich kam nie leer zurück, wenn ich unter Druck und Not Gott gesucht hatte.[20]

The type of evidence her experience brings her, and how she evaluates it, is manifested where she writes:

> How happy I was, that a thousand little incidents in combination proved, as clearly as the drawing of my breath proved me to be living, that I was not without God in the world.

> Wie glücklich war ich, dass tausend kleine Vorgänge zusammen, so gewiss als das Atemholen Zeichen meines Lebens ist, mir bewiesen, dass ich nicht ohne Gott auf der Welt sei.[21]

The image of breathing (Atemholen) illustrates her point.

The aunt sums up her religious experience in personalist terms: 'He was near to me, I was in His presence' (Er war mir nahe, ich war vor ihm).[22] How is this 'presence' to be understood? God's presence to the aunt has to be explained in terms of His transcendence; in what sense can a transcendent being be present to the world He transcends? The only feasible reply is based on the assumption that God is, in the aunt's experience, transcendent in His immanence, as we have explained above.[23] This kind of presence is common to the Old and New Testa-

---

18 *Lehrjahre*, p. 387, 36.
19 Ibid., 20ff.
20 Ibid., 31f.
21 Ibid., 37ff.
22 Ibid., p. 388, 1.
23 Chapter 4.

ments. In the Old Testament, God was present by acting as a force directly shaping the course of His people's history. The exterior manifestation of His transcendent self often took the form of a cloud or a flame of fire. In the New Testament, such signs of His presence were continued, but the central manifestation of God for Christians is Christ Himself: God manifested and present in human flesh. God is understood to be present to the Church through grace. This is not the place for a discussion of the meaning of grace—a long and very involved undertaking beyond the scope of this study. It is sufficient for our purposes to compare the presence of God to an individual person with the presence of two people who have a profound personal relationship with one another based on love.

This latter kind of presence can be considered here under two aspects: firstly, the presence to one another of two people who are not, at a given moment, in one another's company; and secondly, the presence to one another of the same two people when they are in fact in one another's company. It is this latter presence which is the best analogy for describing the type of presence of God to the aunt when she is directly preoccupied with Him (i.e., without any foreground preoccupation with Narziss). The immediacy of the two persons through their physical proximity intensifies the flow of communication and strengthens the bond between them. Between human persons this immediacy depends on physical proximity. In the relationship between God and the aunt there is no question of such dependence, since God Himself is independent of physical conditions of presence.

It is not easy and not necessary to define within what limits God gives Himself in this relationship, i.e., whether or not it is possible for Him to open Himself further, to open essentially more of Himself; whether, for instance, what He shows of Himself now is only the slightest anticipation of what He will show in an after life. Because experience of the latter is not accessible to us we have no means of making such a comparison. In this sense it is not possible for us to say in what God's presence consists.

If we look at the question from the point of view of the effects produced in the aunt by God's presence, we need only refer to her basic sense of security, her peace, strength, autonomy, joy, ethical firmness, confidence in God as her protector—all of which can be summed up as her fulfilment as a person: she finds her true self to the extent that the presence of the divine manifests itself. She accepts herself in the measure that she accepts God. Although the aunt does not speak in these terms, one could analyse the phenomenon as follows: total acceptance of the creator as creator implies total acceptance of oneself (and all others) as creature—both from the positive point of view of all the qualities which are God's creation and from the negative point of view of the limitations inherent in the individual's make-up. Conversely, total acceptance of oneself as creature implies total acceptance of the creator as creator. If one accepts and acknowledges all the positive good that one encounters, one is in fact accepting the work of the creator—all the traces of the creator that one encounters. Above all, if one accepts one's own limitations (and those of others) because one is basically limited, this is to accept the limiting hand of the creator. Thus when the aunt finds her true self she finds God.

9
Faith

In the Narziss episode, the aunt's religious experience gave her strength to carry the responsibility of making and carrying out her decision. The battle for independence and freedom to act according to her own judgments had become more fundamental because it was centred on the very source of her strength: the religious experience itself. Now freedom and autonomy in the religious sphere itself are to form the next step in her gradual development.

In summing up her religious experience (at the time we have been dealing with) in the words: 'He was near to me, I was in His presence' (Er war mir nahe, ich war vor ihm),[1] the aunt is consciously attempting to avoid religious jargon that would identify her as a follower of a theological system. In fact, she would like to have had no theological system at all.[2] But as she says: 'Which of us arrives early at the happiness of being conscious of his individual self, in its pure relationships, without extraneous forms?' (Wer kommt früh zu dem Glücke, sich seines eignen Selbsts, ohne fremde Formen, in reinem Zusammenhang bewusst zu sein?).[3] Only on the way to finding herself, she is naturally prepared to accept help from others, and so: 'I entirely gave in to the Hallean system of conversion.' (ich ergab mich völlig dem Hallischen Bekehrungssystem).[4] She finds, however, that this does not suit her at all. The grades and aspects of religious experience were rigidly prescribed and had little bearing on what she herself has already experienced. 'Deep terror on account of sin' (tiefen Schrecken über die Sünde) was meant to be experienced at the beginning of one's turning

---

1   *Lehrjahre*, p. 388, 1.
2   Ibid., 5.
3   Ibid.
4   Ibid., 9.

to God. This is not at all the case with the aunt. Her experience, as we have seen, has been one in which confidence, peace, joy and inner strength are accentuated. She does eventually come to an awareness of sin in herself and of the need for redemption, but this was not quite the order prescribed by the 'system'. She has enjoyed the positive religious experience (just referred to) for ten years, day in, day out, so that the system seems artificial over against the constancy of her own personal experience:

> This mood of mine continued in me, without change, for half a score of years. It maintained itself through many trials.

> Diese Gemütsbeschaffenheit blieb mir, einen Tag wie den andern, zehn Jahre lang. Sie erhielt sich durch viele Proben.[5]

Her attitude on the death of her mother brings the conflict with the systematizers into the open. Her religious attitude enables her to maintain a basically 'cheerful frame of mind' (heitere Gemütsverfassung) at her mother's death, and this does not fit in at all with the seriousness expected by the 'orthodox people' (schulgerechten Leuten)[6] where an encounter with death was concerned. Challenged by them, she wavers for a while, until she humorously realizes:

> I would have given my life to be distressed and full of fears. But what was my surprise on finding that I absolutely could not. When I thought of God, I was cheerful and contented.

> Ich . . . wäre um mein Leben gern traurig und voll Schrecken gewesen. Wie verwundert war ich aber, da es ein für allemal nicht möglich war! Wenn ich an Gott dachte, war ich heiter und vergnügt.

And she concludes: 'Even at the painful end of my dear mother, I did not shudder at the thought of death' (auch bei meiner lieben Mutter schmerzensvollem Ende graute mir vor dem Tode nicht).[7] Her experience 'in these solemn hours' (in diesen grossen Stunden) makes her more sceptical about other people's insights into these things. She is becoming more reserved, inwardly, in their regard. This manifests itself concretely in her attitude to advice given by her friends in religious matters. She tells one friend she has no need of her advice, and the reason she gives points again to 'what formed the ground of all my conduct' (Grund aller meiner Handlungen): 'I knew my God, and would have no guide but Him' (Ich kenne meinen Gott und wolle ihn ganz

5   Ibid., p. 389, 3f.
6   Ibid., 7.
7   Ibid., 15ff.

allein zum Führer haben).[8] Her decision does not affect just one of her friends. Instead it is a new inner attitude to advice.[9] She is becoming inwardly free in a way that is to enable her to act also outwardly with greater freedom.

> Such determination . . . had the result that also in my temporal affairs I gained sufficient courage to go my own way.

> Dieser Entschluss . . . hatte die Folge, dass ich auch in äusserlichen Verhältnissen meinen eigenen Weg zu gehen Mut gewann.[10]

It is important here to stress, as the aunt does herself, that during this growth towards inner and outer independence her own personal experience of a personal God plays an essential role:

> But for the assistance of my faithful invisible Leader, it could have gone badly with me. I am still astonished at His wise and happy guidance.

> Ohne den Beistand meines treuen unsichtbaren Führers hätte es mir übel geraten können, und noch muss ich über diese weise und glückliche Leitung erstaunen.[11]

Not only does it run counter to any exterior system; it does not involve a system at all—not even one she has invented for herself: 'No one knew how matters stood with me; I did not know myself' (Niemand wusste eigentlich, worauf es bei mir ankam, und ich wusste es selbst nicht).[12]

A further episode brings a very noticeable deepening of her experience. The lack of freedom mentioned where she refers to her inner situation during the Narziss episode is taken up now and treated more explicitly in terms of sin. It is not until the episode we are to deal with now that she has any appreciation at all of this aspect of herself: 'Till now I did not know the thing we call sin' (Das Ding, das man Sünde nennt, kannte ich noch gar nicht).[13] As we saw earlier, it was a certain lack of inner freedom in regard to her environment that made it necessary to withdraw herself. The criterion for judging the opportune moment for withdrawal was the experience of '. . . the sweetest enjoyment of all my powers in my intercourse with my Invisible Friend' (den süssesten Genuss aller meiner Lebenskräfte . . . in dem Umgange mit

8 Ibid., 29.
9 Ibid.
10 Ibid., 32f.
11 Ibid., 35ff.
12 Ibid., 38f.
13 Ibid., p. 390, 4f.

dem unsichtbaren Freunde).[14] For seven years she has lived like this, avoiding situations she is not inwardly free enough to cope with. Meanwhile: 'I perceived, as in a kind of twilight, my weakness and my misery' (ich erkannnte, wie in einer Art von Dämmerung, mein Elend und meine Schwäche). But: 'I did not consider myself bad and thought my state desirable' (ich hielt mich nicht für schlimm und fand meinen Zustand wünschenswert).[15] Still, she is now on the brink of a new discovery about her inner self. A new encounter, this time with a man called Philo,[16] is to bring a new deepening of her religious experience, a new aspect to her relationship to the 'Invisible Friend', and a new freedom and autonomy—both inwardly and outwardly.

The way she enters into the relationship with Philo reveals a pattern we are gradually becoming used to seeing in the aunt's development: 'Contrary to the advice of all my friends, I entered on a new connection' (Gegen den Rat aller meiner Freunde knüpfte ich ein neues Verhältnis an). She hesitates, listening to their advice, but then, influenced by her 'Invisible Leader' (Unsichtbaren Führer)[17] she decides to go ahead 'without fear' (ohne Bedenken). She again sees that her friends' cautions about Philo are not without foundation, and her earlier habit of yielding to others' opinions makes the situation all the more difficult. But her own conviction is too strong and, again helped by her inner religious experience, 'I went forward on my way with reassurance' (so ging ich meinen Pfad getrost fort).[18]

The most immediate significance of the encounter with Philo in the aunt's personal development is the fact that, once she becomes aware of his guilt, she is able, in her identification with him, to focus more clearly on her own inner situation. When she finds out about his guilt, her 'sympathy was lively and complete; I suffered with him; both of us were in the strangest state' (Meine Teilnahme war lebhaft und vollkommen; ich litt mit ihm, und wir befanden uns beide in dem sonderbarsten Zustande).[19] We experience this capacity for self-identification with another as a winning quality in the aunt. It leads her to the discovery: 'You are no better than he' (Du bist nicht besser als er). This thought fills her. It is not merely a passing thought or emotion: 'Nor was it any transitory mood. It lasted for more than a year' (Es war kein schneller

---

14 Ibid., 6f.

15 Ibid., 23.

16 Philo corresponds here to Friedrich Karl von Moser, Susanna von Klettenberg's friend, just as Narziss before him is based on Daniel Olenschlager. See Dechent, *Goethes schöne Seele*, p. 74.

17 *Lehrjahre*, p. 390, 29.

18 Ibid., p. 391, 24.

19 Ibid., p. 392, 9f.

Übergang. Mehr als ein Jahr musste ich [es] empfinden).[20] The experience is not only protracted, but also intense: 'I felt this, and felt it as I
should not wish to do again' (Ich fühlte es und fühlte es so, dass ich es
nicht noch einmal fühlen möchte).[21]

If we find it hard to picture the aunt as a fearful monster like a Girard,
a Cartouche or a Damiens,[22] we can with less hesitation accept her conviction that she needs to be freed 'from this sickness and tendency to
sickness' (von dieser Krankheit und dieser Anlage zur Krankheit).[23] Her
'sickness' is not just the abstract possibility of doing wrong. (This possibility in itself can hardly be called a sickness). Instead, it is a concrete
inner lack of freedom in her orientation to experience as a whole.

Thus the encounter with Philo has the advantage of giving her a new
awareness of her real inner situation. The remaining interest of the episode consists in seeing the growth that gives her the inner liberation she
requires. How is she to heal this 'sickness'?—this is the question uppermost in her mind. What she calls 'practice of virtue' (Tugendübungen) and 'systems of morality' (Sittenlehre) are not promising as means.
The first of them she has already done for years, without even realizing
that she has had the 'sickness' all along! The second she has learned to
look on as totally inferior to the 'fundamental notions which I had
acquired through intercourse with my Invisible Friend' (Grundbegriffe,
die mir der Umgang mit dem unsichtbaren Freunde eingeflösst hatte).[24]
She sees from the Old Testament that her predicament is similar to that
of David, and that he sought a solution through prayer. He wanted to be
'freed from sin' (entsündigt), and he prayed 'earnestly for a pure heart'
(auf das dringendste um ein reines Herz).[25] The aunt's attention becomes
focussed now on Christ and on the message of the New Testament about
faith in Christ. This, she sees, is to be the means of solving her problem;
and so she prays for the sort of faith that will unite her to the Redeemer.

It is important for us to focus on the faith experience that she describes
as following on her prayer. We have to notice above all what she feels
and experiences. (The aunt is not one for offering ingenious theories.
Instead, she stays close to what she directly experiences.) She feels herself inwardly orientated in a new way towards the person Christ. In her

20   Ibid., 18f.
21   Ibid., 17f.
22   Jean Baptiste Girard (1680-1733) was falsely accused of having seduced
     a penitent in confession. Louis Dominique Cartouche (1693-1721) was
     a famous French highwayman. Robert François Damiens (1715-1757)
     is known for his attempt to assassinate Louis XV. See Trunz in his
     notes on the *Lehrjahre*, p. 641.
23   *Lehrjahre*, p. 392, 39f.
24   Ibid., p. 393, 20f.
25   Ibid., 28f.

attempt to communicate this experience, she firstly compares her movement towards Christ with that 'which leads our soul to an absent loved
one' (wodurch unsre Seele zu einem abwesenden Geliebten geführt
wird);[26] secondly, she insists on the convincing quality of the experience
as a real approach to the real person Christ, when she adds: 'A nearing
which perhaps is far more real and true than we imagine' (ein Zunahen,
das vermutlich viel wesentlicher und wahrhafter ist, als wir vermuten).[27]
This inner movement shows her 'what faith was' (was Glauben war).[28]
She says of it further:

> And shortly I became convinced that my soul had acquired a power
> of soaring upwards which was altogether new to it.

> In kurzem war ich überzeugt, dass mein Geist eine Fähigkeit sich
> aufzuschwingen erhalten habe, die ihm ganz neu war.[29]

Since the genuineness of her experience is implicitly called in question
by her milieu, (for example, the uncle), the aunt takes pains to describe
it clearly:

> Words fail us in describing what we feel. I could distinguish them
> most clearly from all fantasy: they were entirely without fantasy,
> without image; yet they gave the same certainty of referring to
> some object as our imagination gives us when it paints the features
> of an absent lover.

> Bei diesen Empfindungen verlassen uns die Worte. Ich konnte sie
> ganz deutlich von aller Phantasie unterscheiden; sie waren ganz
> ohne Phantasie, ohne Bild, und gaben doch eben die Gewissheit
> eines Gegenstandes, auf den sie sich bezogen, als die Einbildungs-
> kraft, indem sie uns die Züge eines abwesenden Geliebten vor-
> malt.[30]

This text, in which the aunt is speaking solely of the religious aspect of
her experience (her relationship to the background element), recalls an
earlier text where she has experienced both background and foreground
elements simultaneously. There, referring to the background aspect, she
has said:

> But the other feeling was not directed towards any form, and yet
> it was unspeakably pleasing.

---

26 Ibid., p. 394, 31f.
27 Ibid., 32f.
28 Ibid., 36.
29 Ibid., 39ff.
30 Ibid., p. 395, 3ff.

Das andere Gefühl bezog sich auf kein Bild und war unaussprechlich angenehm.[31]

This feeling is, in the present text, again referred to as 'not directed
towards any form' (ohne Bild). The phrase in the earlier passage:
'unspeakably pleasing' (unaussprechlich angenehm) has its equivalent
here too: 'Words fail us in describing what we feel' (Bei diesen Empfindungen verlassen uns die Worte). The aunt stresses also: firstly, that the
imagination plays no role in this kind of experience ('without fantasy'
[ohne Phantasie]); secondly, that the experience has the same convincing quality of relationship to an objective reality as an internal image
that a girl has of an absent lover, which represents him to her in his
absence. For the sake of clarity, we might sum up these characteristics of
the aunt's experience of the background aspect as follows:

1 the experience cannot be reduced to words;
2 it is to be distinguished clearly from imaginative experience;
3 it is 'without image' (ohne Bild);
4 it gives a strong impression of being related to objective reality;
5 the aunt's experience of this objective reality can fairly be compared
   with one's experience of an absent lover.[32]

These characteristics help us to distinguish again quite clearly between
foreground and background experience, and the fifth point highlights
the fact that the aunt's background experience has the marks of an
encounter between persons.

The aunt's analysis of her experience of the background conjures up a
broad religious tradition which has its roots in the Bible. The two
phrases 'without fantasy' (ohne Phantasie) and 'without image' (ohne
Bild) remind us perhaps of the Old Testament, where no images of God
were permissible. But in this case the reason for forbidding images seems
to derive, on the one hand, from Yahweh's wish to keep the Israelite cult
absolutely distinct from that of neighbouring peoples who used images,[33]
and on the other, from the dynamic, non-pictorial nature of the Hebrew
mentality which not only was not inclined to the visual arts (sculpture
and painting) but did not think of God in visual images.[34]

But the phrases under discussion seem to have their roots in the
mystical tradition that is more immediate to the *Confession*. There is a
most striking resemblance between these passages and the words of John

31 Ibid., p. 374, 19ff.
32 Ibid., p. 394, 31ff.
33 G. von Rad, *Theologie des Alten Testaments,* vol. 1, (München 1962),
    pp. 230f.
34 Thorleif Boman, *Das Hebräische Denken im Vergleich mit dem Griechi-
    schen* (Göttingen 1965), p. 92.

of the Cross where he speaks about the secret entry of God into the soul.[35] God's approach, in St John's terms, is not through the senses but is a direct contact of spirit with spirit. This contact takes place in the most intimate zone of the person's being where he is not material, where materiality has nothing to say because it has no access to these secret recesses of being. Apart from the fact of the soul's spirituality (=immateriality), St John gives a further reason for the lack of images: on the way towards perfection, the soul is to become more and more convinced that God is all in all; for this reason, God lays the soul's own faculties to rest: the soul is passive while God is active. This passivity is part of the explanation for the fact that the soul's faculties produce no images. It is so passive in this development that it is often hardly aware that the process is going on at all!

Langen quotes a text from Tersteegen:

> And therefore nothing is better than to remain sunk in love's breast without images (bilderlos) and without will (willenlos).[36]

But the term 'bilderlos' is not frequent amongst the pietists. Another expression of the same phenomenon is found in the term 'ineffable',[37] which corresponds to the *ineffabile* of medieval mysticism. In the pietist movement this term was used more loosely than in medieval mysticism and did not refer merely to what was 'ineffable' because hidden in the secrecy of God's being and activity. It was used freely to refer to the most varied human states of soul.[38] When we find it in the *Confession* it is used in a strict sense, in close connection with the experience of contact with the background. The pietists have other more usual expressions for this phenomenon: silence, quiet, rest,[39] which, although adequate to express the state of soul of the mystic in his relation to God, do not however seem intended to express precisely his lack of desire to represent God by any kind of image. This latter mystical attitude is readily traceable to the Spanish mystical tradition of which John of the Cross has served as our example.

This experience, in all its intensity, is what the aunt means by faith. This is what, once and for all, brings her the inner freedom that has been missing. As she is careful to point out, there is no clear break between past and present experience. She realizes

> that my present condition of mind had formerly been known to me; only I had never felt it in such strength.

35　John of the Cross, *Dark Night of the Soul*, II, chapter 8, 5.
36　Langen, *Wortschatz*, p. 42.
37　Ibid., p. 173f.
38　Ibid., p. 174.
39　Ibid., p. 173.

dass mir dieser Zustand der Seele schon vorher bekannt gewesen;
allein ich hatte ihn nie in dieser Stärke empfunden.[40]

It is a difference of degree. Another difference is that 'I had never held
it fast, never made it mine' (Ich hatte ihn niemals festhalten, nie zu eigen
behalten können).[41] But now, after this new experience of faith she has
entered on a new stage, which by contrast with the foregoing period,
brings her a constant strength: instead of experiencing moments of
liberation, she is now once and for all free:

> But now, since that great moment, I had as it were got wings. I
> could mount aloft above what used to threaten me; as the bird can
> fly singing and with ease across the fastest stream, while the little
> dog stands anxiously baying on the bank.

> Nun hatte ich aber seit jenem grossen Augenblicke Flügel bekom-
> men. Ich konnte mich über das, was mich vorher bedrohte, auf-
> schwingen, wie ein Vogel singend über den schnellsten Strom ohne
> Mühe fliegt, vor welchem das Hündchen ängstlich bellend stehen-
> bleibt.[42]

This shows that she has made the transition from the state of lack of
freedom experienced earlier to the state of freedom she has eventually
achieved.

Before moving on to the next (minor) episode, it is worth mentioning
several symptoms which have frequently accompanied the aunt's religious experience. They are mentioned here again in a passage closely
following the one quoted above:

> My joy was indescribable;
> an unaccustomed cheerfulness;
> the reason for my joy;
> the purity of tone in my soul.

> Meine Freude war unbeschreiblich;
> eine ungewöhnliche Heiterkeit;
> die Ursache meines Vergnügens;
> die reine Stimmung in meiner Seele.[43]

These are part of the life and colour of the aunt's experience, and they
are clearly based on her religious experience—her relationship to the
background dimension.

---

40 *Lehrjahre*, p. 395, 9ff.
41 Ibid., 11f.
42 Ibid., 23ff.
43 Ibid., 28ff.

Before having this particularly intense experience of faith, the aunt
has been accustomed to speak freely with others about her inner life. She
would get involved with them and be influenced by their ways of foster-
ing religious experience. This habit continues for a time even afterwards,
though she becomes more aware that the outward forms of expression
used in her environment are of only relative value. For three months
after the experience 'when the truth has been revealed to me' (in welchem
mir das *Wahre* geschenkt worden war),[44] she continues her interest in
external aids to growth in religious experience:

> Images and impressions pointing towards God are presented to us
> by the institutions of the Church, by organs, bells, singing, and
> particularly by the preaching of our pastors.

> Auf Gott zielende Bilder und Eindrücke verschaffen uns kirchliche
> Anstalten, Glocken, Orgeln und Gesänge und besonders die Vor-
> träge unsrer Lehrer.[45]

All this seems to her now quite empty:

> These preachers were blunting their teeth on the shell, while I
> enjoyed the kernel.

> Diese Prediger stumpften sich die Zähne an den Schalen ab, indes-
> sen ich den *Kern* genoss.[46]

Although she finds no satisfaction in and feels inwardly independent of
all that the exterior channels could do for her, she is too used to them to
want to let them go: 'I required images, I wanted external impressions;
and considered it was a purely spiritual desire that I felt' (Bilder wollte
ich haben, äussere Eindrücke bedurfte ich, und glaubte ein reines, geis-
tiges Bedürfnis zu fühlen).[47]

In her contact with the Moravian Brethren and, in particular, with
Count Zinzendorf's writings, she finds something closer to her experience: songs 'which appeared to hint at what I felt' (die . . . auf
dasjenige zu deuten schienen, was ich fühlte). But after further contact
with his writings and his brand of spirituality, she is able to refer to 'the
gimcracks which the Count had stuck round it' (das Tändelwerk, das der
Graf darum gehängt hatte).[48] The 'gimcracks' (Tändelwerk) referred to
included 'the mode of speaking and thinking' (Vorstellungs- und Redens-
arten) of the Brethren, as well as their 'couplets, litanies, and little

---

44   Ibid., p. 397, 17f.
45   Ibid., p. 396, 10ff.
46   Ibid., 30f.
47   Ibid., 34f.
48   Ibid., p. 399, 11f.

pictures' (Verschen, Litaneien und Bildchen). The aunt is soon able to
see that 'few of them could really sense the meaning of the delicate words
and expressions' (nur wenige den Sinn der zarten Worte und Ausdrücke
fühlten), and when she sees a striking concrete example of how they 'in
order to defend an outward form, had almost sacrificed the best that was
in them' (um eine äussere Form zu verteidigen, ihr bestes Innerste
beinahe zerstörten),[49] it costs her little effort 'to lay aside this . . . doll-
work' (das Puppenwerk aus den Händen [zu] legen). Thus we see the
aunt ridding herself of superfluous, insignificant accretions to her religious experience, with the result that she is able, more and more, to
focus on its meaning (Sinn); this means, too, that her inner self (Innerste)
became clearer, less cluttered up. Here we see her in the process of
acquiring the 'purity of existence' (Reinlichkeit des Daseins) attributed
to her by Wilhelm.[50]

49   Ibid., p. 401, 4f.
50   Ibid., p. 518, 11.

10
Transition

We come now to the final main section of the *Confession*. The main function of these pages is to introduce the reader to Natalie's sphere: the world created by the uncle and his collaborator, the Abbé. The aunt remains in the centre of the stage, but various new themes are introduced. The transition comes when the family visits the uncle's house on the occasion of the wedding of the aunt's elder sister. The aunt notes: 'It was the first time in my life, that entering a house aroused admiration in me' (Zum erstenmal in meinem Leben erregte mir der Eintritt in ein Haus Bewunderung).[1] In dealing with the aunt's religious experience, we have seen the inner unity and harmony she was gradually achieving. And now this total confrontation with the world shaped by the uncle's hand is an encounter with something outside herself, which, instead of threatening her inner unity, creates it. Of the music she hears shortly afterwards, she says: 'But now, for the first time, outward things had led me back upon myself' (Nun war ich zum erstenmal durch etwas Äusserliches auf mich selbst zurückgeführt).[2] This 'for the first time' (zum Erstenmal) can be taken to refer to the whole of what she experienced in the house and need not be seen too narrowly in connection with the music as opposed to the architecture. Let us come back to her 'entering the house' (Eintritt in das Haus). She speaks of the

> harmonious impression which I felt . . . and which every hall and chamber deepened.

> den . . . harmonischen Eindruck, den ich beim Eintritt in das Haus empfand, und der sich in jedem Saal und Zimmer verstärkte.[3]

---

1   *Lehrjahre*, p. 401, 35f.
2   Ibid., p. 404, 8ff.
3   Ibid., p. 402, 2ff.

The newness of the experience for her consists mainly in the fact that
she finds this harmony in 'splendour and decoration' (Pracht und Zier-
art). Whereas these have on other occasions only spoiled her inner harmony, she now finds a harmony in them which works actively on herself: 'I felt here concentrated and drawn back upon myself' (so fühlte
ich mich hier gesammelt und auf mich selbst zurückgeführt).[4]

It is important to notice that we have here a correspondence between
an outer harmony incarnated in a work of art (the house) and the inner
harmony it produces in the observer. The unity of the experience is
caused in the first place by a unity found in the 'artist'. This is implied
in the aunt's observation:

> Just as we find it pleasant to see a well-formed person, likewise
> we find pleasure in a whole set-up which betrays the presence of
> an intelligent, reasonable person.

> So angenehm uns der Anblick eines wohlgestalteten Menschen ist,
> so angenehm ist uns eine ganze Einrichtung, aus der uns die Gegen-
> wart eines verständigen, vernünftigen Wesens fühlbar wird.[5]

Thus we have a three-sided correspondence: work, observer, artist. The
same basic harmony is seen under three different aspects as it exists in
the work, affects the observer, stems from the conceiver.

The predominant experience the aunt enjoys in her stay at the uncle's
house is one of unity. The harmony of the architecture is supported by a
further tuning in of furniture and table-ware:

> The furniture, plate, table-ware, and table ornaments accorded
> with the general whole; and if in other houses you would say the
> architect has been at the same school as the pastry-cook, it here
> appeared as if even our pastry-cook and butler had taken lessons
> from the architect.

> Aller Hausrat, Tafelzeug, Service und Tischaufsätze stimmten zu
> dem Ganzen, und wenn mir sonst die Baumeister mit den Kondi-
> toren aus einer Schule entsprungen zu sein schienen, so war hier
> Konditor und Tafeldecker bei dem Architekten in die Schule
> gegangen.[6]

This unity is not limited to the house and its furnishings, but is extended
to the arrangements for entertaining the guests:

---

4   Ibid., 6.
5   Ibid., p. 403, 29ff.
6   Ibid., p. 402, 28ff.

In like manner, the preparations for these celebrations and festivities produced a silent pleasure, by their air of dignity and splendour; and to me it seemed as incomprehensible that one man could have invented and arranged all this, as that more than one could have worked together on so high a level.

Auch in allen Anstalten zu Feierlichkeiten und Festen erregten Pracht und Würde ein stilles Gefallen, und es war mir ebenso unbegreiflich, dass ein Mensch das alles hätte erfinden und anordnen können, als dass mehrere sich vereinigen könnten, um in einem so grossen Sinne zusammenzuwirken.[7]

This direct experience of a unifying spirit (in this case, that of the uncle) is the concretization of what the uncle goes on to discuss in abstract terms in his conversations with his niece. He speaks of a creative power which lies deep in us and is capable of producing 'what is meant to be' (das . . . , was sein soll).[8] Our task can be something to be achieved in ourselves (an uns) or outside ourselves. In condescension (at least in his manner of speaking) to his niece, he says she has perhaps chosen the better part: 'making your moral being, your deep, loving nature harmonise with itself and with God' (Ihr sittliches Wesen, Ihre tiefe, liebevolle Natur mit sich selbst und mit dem höchsten Wesen übereinstimmend zu machen).[9] She has worked at and achieved an inner harmony with herself, based on a more fundamental harmony with God (dem höchsten Wesen), or the 'Invisible Friend', as we have seen above. Over against this kind of unity, which is characterized to a large extent by a certain independence with regard to the external world, the uncle proposes as a complement the one which he himself strives for:

. . . to get acquainted with all the complexity of man on the sense level and to bring about an active harmony.

. . . den sinnlichen Menschen in seinem Umfange zu kennen und tätig in *Einheit* zu bringen suchen.[10]

(This latter kind of unity corresponds to that experienced in the house, and referred to by the aunt where she speaks of the 'spirit of a higher culture though one which is limited to the level of sense' (Geist einer höhern, obgleich auch nur sinnlichen Kultur).[11]

From the text we can see that the two kinds of unity are not merely meant to exist side by side (i.e., in different persons), but can be found

---

7   Ibid., 7ff.
8   Ibid., p. 405, 18f.
9   Ibid., 22ff.
10 Ibid., 25ff.
11 Ibid., p. 403, 37f.

in one and the same person and thus constitute a fuller, more resonant harmony.

The uncle's kind of harmony is brought into closer relation to that of his niece when he shows her a series of paintings chosen to illustrate the various stages of formation to be undergone before

> the man of genius can move gaily and freely on the pinnacle, the very sight of which makes us giddy.

> das Genie auf dem Gipfel, bei dessen blossem Anblick uns schwindelt, sich frei und fröhlich bewege.[12]

The aunt's immediate reaction is to compare this kind of achievement with 'moral culture' (die moralische Bildung). The uncle takes up this idea and proceeds to show how this kind of 'culture' (Bildung)—the aunt's—should not be promoted in isolation from the artistic kind he has been discussing. He maintains that

> he whose spirit strives for a development of that kind, has likewise every reason, at the same time, to improve his finer powers of sense.

> dass derjenige, dessen Geist nach einer moralischen Kultur strebt, alle Ursache hat, seine feinere Sinnlichkeit zugleich mit auszubilden.[13]

Here we see the two harmonies required of the one person. Next comes the reason why the 'moral' harmony is not sufficient by itself: because of the danger

> of sinking from his moral height, by giving way to the enticements of a lawless fancy, and degrading his moral nature by allowing it to take delight in tasteless baubles, if not something worse.

> von seiner moralischen Höhe herabzugleiten, indem er sich den Lockungen einer regellosen Phantasie übergibt und in den Fall kommt, seine edlere Natur durch Vergnügen an geschmacklosen Tändeleien, wo nicht an etwas Schlimmerem herabzuwürdigen.[14]

The word 'baubles' (Tändeleien) hits home, reminding the aunt of her own very recent past. She has rejected the 'tasteless baubles' (Tändeleien) because they were a distraction from 'what is true' (das Wahre). The uncle would reject them for a different reason, precisely because they were 'tasteless' (geschmacklos) and not worthy of the aunt's 'finer nature' (edlere Natur).

The uncle's words point to a weakness in her position. Even if she is

---

12   Ibid., p. 408, 21ff.

13   Ibid., 31ff.

14   Ibid., 34ff.

no longer caught up in the 'baubles' (Tändeleien), the question still remains whether she has sufficiently developed her 'finer sensibility' (feinere Sinnlichkeit) or whether this is something lacking in her. In fact, contact with the uncle's world has made her aware of real shortcomings in herself. As we saw above,[15] here for the first time contact with the outside world brought her to reflection on herself. This suggests that in her adjustment to the world around her there is need of further development. Comparing herself with Natalie, her niece, the aunt says that she treated poor people in a far less personal way (than Natalie did), giving them money and, in a sense, buying herself free. If they were not related to her, she tended to look on her care of them merely as part of a duty to be absolved. This points to a narrowing off of contact with persons in the outside world. A further example to suggest that her attitude has been too narrow is found in her own discoveries about vocal music. The glorious music presented by the uncle gave them

> if I may say so, a real foretaste of bliss. Till then, I had known only the pious mode of singing, as good souls practise it, frequently with hoarse throats, imagining, like wild birds, that they are praising God, because what they do gives them a pleasant feeling themselves.

> ich darf wohl sagen, wirklich einen Vorschmack der Seligkeit. . . . Ich hatte bisher nur den frommen Gesang gekannt, in welchem gute Seelen oft mit heiserer Kehle, wie die Waldvögelein, Gott zu loben glauben, weil sie sich selbst eine angenehme Empfindung machen.[16]

The relevance of real art for her religious experience has always escaped her, whether on the visual or aural plane. (She brackets concert music of a showy kind, in so far as it is directed towards highlighting a particular talent rather than communicating in depth.) But now she is confronted with

> . . . music, which, as it originated from the most accomplished human beings, was, by suitable and practised organs in harmonious unity, made again to address the deepest and best feelings of man, and to impress him at that moment with a lively sense of his likeness to God.

> Musik, aus dem tiefsten Sinne der trefflichsten menschlichen Naturen entsprungen, die durch bestimmte und geübte Organe in harmonischer Einheit wieder zum tiefsten, besten Sinne des Menschen sprach und ihn wirklich in diesem Augenblicke seine Gottähnlichkeit lebhaft empfinden liess.[17]

15 See beginning of chapter 10.
16 *Lehrjahre*, p. 410, 33ff.
17 Ibid., p. 411, 2ff.

From this text we can see that music, as experienced in this particular case, is closely linked with the experience we have been studying in the *Confession*. Various elements already highlighted recur here. We have again the three-way relationship set up between the source of the work of art (here: composer), the observer (here: listener) and the work itself. This music arises 'from deep down' (aus dem tiefsten Sinne), in its execution it appears 'in harmonious unity' (in harmonischer Einheit), and it speaks to 'the deepest and best feelings of man' (zum tiefsten, besten Sinne des Menschen). The inner core of the person is involved in an encounter with reality distinct from himself; the medium of the experience (the executed work of art) is the centre of focus, and an accompanying aspect of the experience is that it allows the person 'at that moment a lively sense of his likeness to God' (in diesem Augenblicke seine Gottähnlichkeit lebhaft empfinden). This latter aspect ties in with the background experience we have encountered constantly, and it is seen here in company with the intense foreground focus. And when she says, in the continuation of the passage on music:

> They were all devotional songs, in the Latin language; . . . and without pretending to edify, they elevated me and made me happy in the highest manner,

> Alles waren lateinische geistliche Gesänge, die . . . mich, ohne Anforderung einer sogenannten Erbauung, auf das geistigste erhoben und glücklich machten,[18]

she seems to have perceived the possibility of a higher unity: between religious experience and experience of real art, in which the insistence on a so-called edification was to diminish. Perhaps, by learning to see the role of genuine art and putting aside the insipid songs and pictures she has allied with her religious experience, she is on the way to a still more genuine religious attitude. But it is at most a beginning. The difficulty is: 'For a pictorial form to mean anything to me, it should instruct, affect, improve me' (So sollte mir auch eine bildliche Darstellung etwas sagen, sie sollte mich belehren, rühren, bessern).[19] The uncle obviously tried to foster in her a broader interest in the works of art by explaining them in letters. But, as she says, despite all his efforts, 'it was always the same for me' (so blieb es mit mir doch immer beim alten).

Yet another important line of development is opened up for the

---

18   Ibid., 7ff.
19   Ibid., p. 412, 3f.

aunt, but we have no opportunity of seeing if the growth takes place. Her father's attitude at death gives yet another support to her religious conviction: she speaks of his 'cheerfulness' (Heiterkeit) and 'lively joy' (lebhaften Freude).[20] Here is her summing up of what this experience means for her religiously:

> No arguments will ever convince me that a higher power was not visibly at work.

> Die sichtbaren Wirkungen einer höhern Kraft dabei wird mir niemand wegräsonieren.[21]

Her father's death has a further impact on her. She finds herself with time on her hands and leisure to think about the prospect of death. In connection with this she says:

> It (her soul) looked upon the body as a foreign substance, as we look upon a garment.

> Sie (die Seele) sah den Körper selbst als ein ihr fremdes Wesen an, wie man etwa ein Kleid ansieht.[22]

How are we meant to evaluate this clear distinction she draws between body and soul? The clue is found in the advice given her by the uncle's house doctor, who fits harmoniously into the uncle's world, where there is no place for a radical body-soul dualism. The doctor points out to the aunt that she is in real danger of inner self-destruction if in her experience of transitoriness she turns in on herself. Her conviction that 'the body too will be torn like a garment' (der Körper wird wie ein Kleid zerreissen)[23] can genuinely be interpreted as meaning that she experiences herself as being a person whose reality is not destroyed in death: 'I, the self I know so well, I exist' (Ich, das wohlbekannte Ich, Ich bin).[24] There would, in fact, come a time when her reality would not even partly consist in the corporal aspect of herself. This means there must be at least some distinction possible between herself (ich) and what could one day be destroyed in death. The doctor's advice helps her to avoid living as though the distinction were already sharply drawn within herself—as if the self were in fact here and now living in absolute autonomy with regard to all that is transitory around it. The doctor's role is, in terms which smack of the uncle's

20 Ibid., p. 413, 29f.
21 Ibid., 37f.
22 Ibid., p. 415, 21f.
23 Ibid., 26.
24 Ibid., 27.

pedagogy, to show her how to avoid this fatal hollowing out of herself. He says:

> To be active . . . is the primary vocation of man; all the intervals
> in which he is obliged to rest he should employ in gaining clear
> knowledge of external things, for this will afterwards facilitate his
> activity.

> Tätig zu sein . . . ist des Menschen erste Bestimmung, und alle
> Zwischenzeiten, in denen er auszuruhen genötigt ist, sollte er
> anwenden, eine deutliche Erkenntnis der äusserlichen Dinge zu
> erlangen, die ihm in der Folge abermals seine Tätigkeit erleich-
> tert.[25]

What is obvious from this text is his attempt to turn her gaze out-
wards, away from herself, to attempt an encounter with the rest of
creation. The aunt writes that the doctor

> led me up and down as if in Paradise; . . . allowing me to sense
> remotely the Creator walking in the Garden in the cool of the
> evening.

> führte mich wie im Paradiese umher, und . . . liess mich den in
> der Abendkühle im Garten wandelnden Schöpfer aus der Entfer-
> nung ahnen.[26]

The doctor's advice thus leads her to a new discovery parallel to that
of her art experience. He has helped her open out to the exterior
world here designated as 'nature' (Natur), which is to be the new
component with her religious experience:

> How gladly did I now see God in nature, when I bore Him with
> such certainty within my heart! How interesting to me was His
> handiwork; how thankful did I feel that He had pleased to
> quicken me with the breath of His mouth.

> Wie gerne sah ich nunmehr Gott in der Natur, da ich ihn mit
> solcher Gewissheit im Herzen trug, wie interessant war mir das
> Werk seiner Hände, und wie dankbar war ich, dass er mich mit
> dem Atem seines Mundes hatte beleben wollen.[27]

We have here another beginning which shows that, in principle, her
religious experience is not a cramped one, but can be synthesized with
a broad range of further experiences. The *Confession* does not go far
enough to allow us to judge whether the aunt's growth along these two

25 Ibid., 36ff.
26 Ibid., p. 416, 11ff.
27 Ibid., 15ff.

new paths of integration really took place or not. Given her feeble
health and the fact that her role is shown to be quite secondary to that
of the fully integrated Natalie, we have not much reason to believe
that this growth actually took place. But it is at least shown as possible. The closing pages of the *Confession* show us that the basic inner
maturity has been achieved and that from this inner core a growth is
beginning which should lead to fuller and deeper contact with the
outside world. We are reminded here of the interpretation given to
Wilhelm's own experience, when Goethe says:

> He knew not that it is the manner of all persons who attach im-
> portance to their interior growth to neglect their outward circum-
> stances altogether.

> Er wusste nicht, dass es die Art aller der Menschen sei, denen an
> ihrer innern Bildung viel gelegen ist, dass sie die äusseren Ver-
> hältnisse ganz und gar vernachlässigen.[28]

The parallel between the aunt's and Wilhelm's experience in this
regard is striking.

---

28 Ibid., p. 491, 33ff.

II
Conclusion of the Confession

The conclusion of the *Confession* shows the aunt making way for the new world which is to dominate the rest of the novel. In the last few pages of the *Confession* we are introduced to the generation which, along with Wilhelm, is under the Abbé's and the uncle's tutelage. In Natalie the aunt sees herself eclipsed. There is a deep bond between them and Natalie resembles her aunt in many respects. But Natalie has qualities which the aunt does not possess in any full way.

The eclipse occurs also on a second level: it becomes clear that the uncle, who is responsible for the education of the children, intends to keep the children away from his niece: 'That my uncle keeps them from me, I endure with patience' (Ich ertrage es mit Geduld, dass der Oheim sie von mir entfernt hält).[1]

The reason behind this is that the uncle thinks her dangerous for the children's education. He is clearly determined to educate them according to his own bent, so that exposure to the outside world is emphasized even to the exclusion of the 'acquaintance with themselves and with the invisible, sole, faithful Friend' (dem Umgange mit sich selbst und mit dem unsichtbaren, einzigen treuen Freunde)[2] and, since even Natalie has no apparent rapport with the aunt's inner world—

> she showed not the . . . smallest need, of a dependence upon any visible or invisible Being
>
> sie liess . . . kein Bedürfnis einer Anhänglichkeit an ein sichbares oder unsichtbares Wesen . . . auf irgendeine Weise merken,[3]

—the aunt's eclipse looks all the more complete.

---

1   *Lehrjahre,* p. 419, 11f.
2   Ibid., 35f.
3   Ibid., 2ff.

But the eclipse may be less real than apparent, as a detailed study of Natalie's attitude might well show. In any case, the *Confession* concludes with the aunt's reaffirming her conviction of 'the reality of my belief' (der Realität meines Glaubens).[4] No one could argue away her firm conviction since it is based on her own inner experience and has a real practical influence on her life. (See especially the decision-making discussed in earlier pages.) Although she feels herself pushed into the background, she suffers no inner defeat. The inner achievement that she attributes to her religious experience is referred to forcibly where she says

> that I am still advancing, never going back; that my conduct is approximating more and more to the image I have formed of perfection; that I every day feel more facility in doing what I reckon proper, even while the weakness of my body so obstructs . . . I scarcely remember a commandment; to me there is nothing that assumes the aspect of law; it is an impulse that leads me, and guides me always rightly. I freely follow my emotions, and know as little of constraint as of repentance.

> dass ich immer vorwärts, nie rückwärts gehe, dass meine Handlungen immer mehr der Idee ähnlich werden, die ich mir von der Vollkommenheit gemacht habe, dass ich täglich mehr Leichtigkeit fühle, das zu tun, was ich für recht halte, selbst bei der Schwäche meines Körpers, der mir so manchen Dienst versagt: . . . Ich erinnere mich kaum eines Gebotes, nichts erscheint mir in Gestalt eines Gesetzes, es ist ein Trieb, der mich leitet und mich immer recht führet; ich folge mit Freiheit meinen Gesinnungen und weiss so wenig von Einschränkung als von Reue.[5]

---

4   Ibid., p. 420, 5.
5   Ibid., 13ff.

12
Conclusion

Having completed our analysis of the aunt's experience we can now attempt to summarize the conclusions to be drawn from it. These fall quite naturally into four groups corresponding to each of our four introductory chapters, i.e. concerning (1) the 'schöne Seele' as such; (2) the relationship of this particular kind of experience to the sentimentalist movement; (3) its relationship to the pietist movement; and (4) the literary re-evaluation of the role of the aunt (as 'schöne Seele').

In our early comments about the 'schöne Seele' as it appears in Goethe's writings, we needed to stress the fact that Goethe himself was not interested in creating a 'schöne Seele' that would measure up to any fixed definition. Goethe was not working with any fixed definition of 'schöne Seele'. What interested him was to reproduce an instance of the phenomenon known to him in his experience. The 'schöne Seele' of the *Confession* was to be an individual representing a particular type of person. It is this phenomenon that we have been attempting to describe and analyse. To round off our study we need to give a brief synthesis of our findings in this regard.

The 'schöne Seele' we find in the *Confession* manifests most of the characteristics revealed by a study of the history of 'schöne Seele': if, in the *Confession*, the beautiful and the good are not completely identical as they are for Plotinus, there is at least a close link between the two. The harmony found in the aunt's experience, between the background and foreground elements, is the foundation for the beauty of soul we find in her; more accurately, her beauty consists in this harmony. In one sense it can be said that this harmony is also what constitutes her goodness: complete consonance with the background element (seen as divine) is equal to basic goodness. This latter is a state of inner being which has resulted at least partly from ethical striving. Once basically achieved, this inner state forms the basis for further ethical judgments and 'good' actions. These ethically good actions will reinforce the basic harmony making the person more thoroughly good and more thoroughly beautiful. The 'good' actions may also be 'beautiful' if they serve to radiate and manifest the inner beauty. On the other hand, it is clear that in the sphere of activity good and beautiful are not identical: ethical actions are extensions of basic goodness into the conscious life of the person where his activities are determined to some extent by his judgments. These latter, even in the case of a basically 'good' person, can be erroneous. A series of actions based on erroneous judgments are not bad themselves and do not make the person bad; on the other hand they might show an ugly dissonance with the basic harmony, and therefore can hardly be called beautiful. It follows that whereas beauty and goodness in Goethe's 'schöne Seele' are closely related, they are not wholly identical because the basic harmony, when being radiated through one's conscious activity, can be somewhat distorted in such a way that the good and the beautiful part company. I suggest that the reason why the critics treat Natalie's aunt severely is that their attention has been focussed principally on the external sphere of her activities where she has definite limitations: unlike Natalie, she is not personally attuned to the needs of people outside a very small circle of her own; furthermore, her concrete attitude towards nature and art, while showing a certain openness and promise of development, leaves much to be desired. But to concentrate on such limitations is to miss precisely the aspect of her experience which warranted the inclusion of the *Confession* in the *Apprenticeship:* the profound inner harmony which made a deep impression on Wilhelm and contributed to his growth and development.

The stress laid by the Latin stoics on equilibrium, harmony, firmness and constancy in their conception of 'schöne Seele' is repeated in Goethe's 'schöne Seele'; our analysis of the structure of the aunt's experience has been able to indicate the basis for such qualities, thus giving an ultimate explanation for their presence in her. What is the ultimate basis in the stoic experience is a further question which does not concern us here. It is sufficient to note that these qualities found in the stoic 'schöne Seele' recur in Goethe's 'schöne Seele', supported by the basic background experience in a way that is characteristic of Natalie's aunt.

The link with the Augustinian and medieval mystical tradition has also become quite obvious. The fundamental experience of God in this tradition brought a new element to the beauty of the soul. The soul's beauty was enhanced by its contact with the grace of God. With Natalie's aunt, her inner life centred on the presence of the 'Invisible Friend'; the constancy of this presence gave her the constant experience of the background dimension, the foundation of her existence. It was with this background experience that all else had to harmonize in her inner life. The most obvious sign of the link between the 'schöne Seele' of the *Confession* and the early mystical tradition is the importance given to the spouse imagery which has its origin in the *Canticle of Canticles.*

The Canticle imagery links the *Confession* also with the modern Spanish mystical tradition, a further link being the stress on the *lack of images* to correspond to the soul's direct experience of God.[1]

One of the main reasons for undertaking the study of the 'schöne Seele' of the *Confession* is that it can serve as a preliminary study aimed at shedding light on the experience of Natalie, who is the most perfect example of the phenomenon. Other examples whom it would be significant to study in order to complete one's picture of the Goethean conception of the type would be Iphigenie and the Princess (in *Tasso*). We have already drawn attention to the links between Natalie and her aunt, and it is reasonable to suppose that there is profound continuity between the experience of each of them.

The problem that would arise for a detailed study of the relationships between the aunt and Natalie is perhaps best explained in terms of a process of secularization which took place as Goethe developed. The time of his exposure to pietism was the pre-Weimar period, 1768-1775. This is the time in which he fell under the direct influence of Susanna von Klettenberg, Theodor Lange and Johann Caspar Lavater. He came to grips with Christianity in a serious way, and, as Emil Staiger writes:

> Goethe himself, as we know, wrote his most genuine work first of all in pietist language. The lyric poetry written in Strasbourg and Frankfurt would be unthinkable without the words *Fülle, Strom, Stille, innig, rein, sich öffnen* and *verschliessen*, words which, along with many others only derived the full weight of their meaning from the eloquence of the pietists.[2]

The *Confession* was written twenty years later when Goethe had considerably drawn back from Christianity; at this time he no longer accepted it as a revealed religion; but his basic respect for religion is still evident from the role of honour given to the pastor in *Hermann und Dorothea* (1797); from the *Prologue in Heaven* (1800) and the final scene of *Faust* (1830), where the hero is saved; from the person of Ottilie and her holiness, which Goethe seems to take quite seriously (1809); and finally from Goethe's preoccupation with mysticism as we find it in the person of Makarie in the *Wanderjahre* (1821 on-

---

1 See above, p. 82ff.
2 Staiger, *Goethe*, p. 140.

wards). Despite a marked cooling of his enthusiasm for Christianity, Goethe is still able to produce the 'schöne Seele' and, what is perhaps even more significant, Natalie. Goethe wrote to Schiller (18 August 1795): 'I do not let the Christian religion appear in its purest form until the eighth book, in a later generation'.

For Goethe himself, Natalie is a purer manifestation of Christianity than even her aunt! This seems to indicate Goethe's conviction that the Christian experience from the aunt to her niece Natalie, despite all appearances of a process of secularization, involves an organic continuity in which the experience in Natalie's case is more Christian than that of her pietist aunt! However the process of secularization is to be understood, it does not seem to imply that the Christian experience contained in the *Apprenticeship* will be stripped of any essential dimensions. Goethe's own comments invite us to undertake a further study, in which the aim would be to show the continuity of the same background-foreground structure in Natalie's and her aunt's experience, the same harmonious structure which supports the life, joy, serenity, constancy and sense of purpose which we have been studying in these pages. The text of the novel itself would be used as the ultimate test of this continuity.

In the introduction[3] we posed the question whether the aunt's experience was only a 'manifestation of the sentimentality of the eighteenth century which could not survive except as a literary curiosity, a psychological aberration'. From our brief introductory survey (chapter 2) we saw that to identify the aunt's experience with that typical of sentimentalism would imply a negative judgment of the value of her experience.

Her experience is not that of the 'naïve' person who fits naturally and without conscious effort into her surroundings. Any harmony she achieved in herself and with her milieu cost her the struggle of overcoming tensions. On the other hand, she was not 'sentimental', but, in Wieser's terminology 'sentimentalisch'. If one reads the *Confession* with a knowledge of eighteenth-century sentimentalism and yet does not carefully distinguish between two quite distinct phenomena—the experience termed 'sentimentalisch' and the one termed 'sentimental' —the door is open to the misunderstandings typical of criticism concerning Natalie's aunt.

We saw in the introductory section[4] that even Natalie's gentle criticism of her aunt was not substantiated by the text of the *Confession* itself. Close analysis of the text has shown the aunt's vigour and inner vitality, her strength and moral courage, her positive attitude

---

3 See above, p. 7.
4 See above, p. 10.

towards creation as opposed to an attitude marked by ressentiment; we have seen that her preoccupation with herself was a function of self-understanding, a prerequisite for adjusting to difficult circumstances—and not, as Natalie would have it, 'perhaps too much preoccupation with herself'. Furthermore, what Natalie called her 'moral and religious scrupulosity' can at most be an interpretation which Natalie puts on her aunt's experience but which is not at all borne out by what we find in the text of the *Confession*. Perhaps the inconsistency between what Natalie says and what is evident in the *Confession* is to be attributed to Goethe himself (who has shown himself in *Faust*, for instance, quite capable of such inconsistencies); but it is above all the text itself and the experience it expresses that are of prime importance to us. Our analysis has shown that the aunt has a sensitive, delicate conscience which reflects a keen awareness of values and purpose in her life rather than an anxious state of insecurity and indecision. 'Scrupulosity' is an expression that does the aunt complete injustice. What is stressed is the 'Grund aller meiner Handlungen'. The whole trend of the *Confession* is for the aunt to become more acutely aware of this background dimension and, accordingly, to become more sure of herself and to banish all fear.

The effect of her illness can easily prejudice our judgment of her unless we examine it closely. In our analysis we have shown how the illness worked in a positive way by turning her thoughts to the 'Invisible Friend'. The impartial observer of such a phenomenon would say that her sickness was the occasion of her taking interest in God. An observer who is totally sceptical about a divine reality would look on such an interest as an illusory attitude produced by sickness, or as a manifestation of a psychological aberration corresponding to the physical disorder. It is not our task here to refute such presuppositions in themselves but to propose the interpretation—as we have done—that the text itself seems to warrant. The way the aunt describes her experience suggests the more positive interpretation. She introduces the theme of sickness mainly to show it as one of the principal factors which helped her (as occasions can help, without being causes) in her orientation towards the 'Invisible Friend'. (The really decisive steps in her religious development were made in connection with the love episodes concerning Narziss and Philo—and here sickness plays no part at all!) She herself is convinced of the existence of a divine reality; thus from her point of view there would be nothing deserving of reproach even if sickness were the main factor inducing her preoccupation with God. If sickness can put her in more profound touch with reality, then sickness itself can be seen in a positive light: namely as a medium through which God can communicate with the human person; this basic conviction is poles apart from the sceptical view that a sick person creates

God as a psychological crutch which is as artificial as the wooden one used to support the frail body. But on the point of God's reality, the aunt has no need to argue: God imposes Himself as real, as a personal force confronting her at every turn.

From our analysis of the text it should now be clear that whatever negative judgments might be passed on the aunt we are not justified in identifying her with the negative side of eighteenth-century sentimentalism.

In addition to what was already evident from Langen's work, namely that the language and theme of the *Confession* are typically pietist, we have been able to see, also with regard to the experience of the 'schöne Seele', that it is more cognate with pietism than with the sentimentalism of the eighteenth century.

In the aunt there is the subjectivism found in the pietist's reliance on his own inner experience and feeling rather than on any external authority. Yet this feeling is not valued for its own sake, as feeling is with the sentimentalists. Instead, it serves as a criterion that the relationship between God and the person is positive. The relationship itself is of primary importance, and feeling, as a criterion, is subordinate to it. The 'schöne Seele' dwells on her experience of the friendship with God and with Christ, but her subjectivity is not thrown back on itself: it is involved with a real structure outside herself—with a background element, whose influence predominates in her life, and a foreground element, which, as we have seen, is taken seriously in its own right, even though in fact her life is not able to develop very considerably in the foreground sphere.

We have seen that the *Confession* is a kind of autobiography. It reveals the typically pietist preoccupation with one's own inner life. The 'schöne Seele' shows a remarkable gift not only for expressing her experience, but also for expressing it analytically. Her powers of psychological observation are considerable. Her differentiated grasp of experience (in which background and foreground are in harmony, but not confused) is superior to that of Novalis in the poem referred to in the introduction.[5]

In her attitude towards sin, her position represents a strong modification of pietism. She has a positive view of creation, though, as we have seen, she has room for extensive development in this sphere of experience. What is important to retain is that in principle she is open to such development. She is not closed off in a small circle of 'beloved ones' whose whole life consists of being charitable to one another. Such an attitude would leave little room for the exterior (secular) world, whereas the aunt at least sees the importance of extending her horizon.

---

5 See above, p. 22f.

Her calmness and trust in God's providence is quite typical of
pietism, but here we have seen the basis on which it rests. The general
pietist attitude showed signs of insecurity: the search for exterior
signs of God's favour. There was none of this with the 'schöne Seele'.
If she was sensitive to manifestations of God's presence and favour,
she did not pounce on them to use them as proof of the validity of her
religious experience. They quietly confirmed the inner certainty she
had of God's presence, a certainty which was not exclusively interior
but based, as well, on the fact that her conviction helped her face the
crises she was confronted with in real life: for example, the decision
she had to make concerning Narziss and the pressures she had to
overcome to live her own life.

Yet in her general attitude to created being she reflected the imma-
nentism of the pietists as opposed to the otherworldliness of the Calvinists.[6] Her striving for self-perfection is typical of pietism: it is
based on a conviction of the person's own value. In the 'schöne Seele'
this conviction seems to have developed beyond the stage of merely
seeing Christ as the only good in the person towards a more Goethean
stage in which the person is optimistically seen as of absolutely positive value. Perhaps here, as well as in her attitude towards sin, the
aunt's pietism has been modified to suit Goethe's taste and his literary
intention of creating a character who could serve as a positive educative influence on his hero, Wilhelm.

An investigation of the kind we have been attempting ultimately
demands a confrontation with the critical literature already written
about the *Apprenticeship*. The most immediate difficulty one sees in
this is the sheer volume of work that has been done. Yet there is a
considerable difference in the amount of attention that has been paid
to a work like *Faust* and the less popular *Wilhelm Meister*. Then, if
one focusses on the sixth book of the *Apprenticeship* one is surprised
to see how little attention it has attracted.

No analysis of the kind we have presented has been attempted.
Authors who see the *Confession* in a positive light refer to it as one
of the formative influences to which Wilhelm is exposed; they say a
few words about its function of introducing Wilhelm gradually to the
classical world of Natalie and then they pass on to a consideration
of the seventh and eighth books.

The person who seems to have had most to say in favour of the
aunt is Friedrich Gundolf in his monumental work on Goethe. In his
chapter on the *Apprenticeship*, Gundolf says that the figures introduced into the novel as additions to those already in the *Vocation to
the Theatre* are, by comparison to these, merely allegories whose

---

6 See above, chapter 3.

presence in the novel is due to the needs of the total conception of the work (Gesamtidee). Thus, with characters like Natalie, Therese and Lothario, Goethe's joy in creating really individual characters has gone, and he is only creating representatives (Vertreter) of his ideas.[7] It is important to note that he adds, with reference to the aunt, who is also one of the new characters, that 'she is perhaps an exception'[8] to this rule. Gundolf's comments about the later part of the novel are not to be taken as negative criticism. He says himself, with regard to Goethe's aim in the novel, that the *Apprenticeship* is not meant to portray individuals and passions but to present educative processes, inner attitudes, layers of experience and atmospheres.[9] The persons themselves, apart from those of the earlier *Vocation to the Theatre*, are only introduced and portrayed in so far as they are needed for the purpose of presenting educative processes and inner attitudes.[10] Of all the new characters, the one least affected by this, according to Gundolf, is the 'schöne Seele', because she is a portrait of the soul, a quiet development of an inner disposition.[11] Gundolf implies that the life she manifests is not to be sought in gesture, action and conversation.[12] This fact preserves her from sharing the fate of the other 'new' characters who, because their 'life' is not so 'interior', must convince us of their liveliness by the external means mentioned: gesture, action and conversation; and it is precisely these features that Goethe has suppressed in books seven and eight, with the result that the characters become shadowy.[13] (If we were dealing directly with books seven and eight, much would need to be said to modify Gundolf's appraisal of these characters. But we can pass over it.)

Gundolf refers to the various milieux to which Wilhelm is exposed, milieux which contribute towards his education. Each of these has two aspects: its own reality and value, plus an unconscious function in educating Wilhelm. It is the latter of these that the critics have been concerned with. Very little attention has been paid to the former (with the inevitable result, as an examination of criticism relating to books seven and eight would show, that the real effect of the *Confession* on Wilhelm is hardly noticed at all, or is at least minimized.) It has been our task here to draw attention to and to analyse what Gundolf refers to as the peculiar force (Eigengewicht) and peculiar colour

---

7 Gundolf, *Goethe*, p. 517.
8 Ibid.
9 Ibid., p. 518.
10 Ibid.
11 Ibid., p. 517.
12 Ibid.
13 Ibid., p. 518.

(Eigenfarbe)[14] of this particular milieu. Gundolf himself is accurate in referring to this aspect of the *Confession:* he refers to book six as the presentation of the purely contemplative life and goes on to say:

> Along with so many who are involved in serious active work, or who are consciously striving to attain a goal, or are wandering aimlessly; along with those who, with or without dignified and noble aims, are busy, ambitious, commanding, serving, enjoying, wandering, desiring—alongside these the portrait of the contemplative must take its place, a form of experience not missing in Goethe's own existence and imprinted on his mind as a memory of Susanna von Klettenberg . . . the *vita contemplativa* as an essential aspect of education is indispensable in the *Bildungsroman.*[15]

As far as it goes, this general assessment of the 'schöne Seele's' particular form of experience is accurate. But a detailed analysis of the *Confession* would have helped to avoid judgments like the one implied in the phrases: 'through turning away from the world to a purely harmonious inner life'[16] and 'that she has seen through the valuelessness or appearance of value of earthly things'.[17] Our detailed analysis of the *Confession* has shown that judgments like these do not survive confrontation with the text itself. The phrase in which he refers to her preoccupation as hovering in the pure contemplation of the divinity[18] is found to be equally misleading when measured against the text: Gundolf in no way indicates the role of the foreground in the aunt's experience; whereas it is important not only to see that it has a role, but also to define, as we have done, its relationship to the background element in the transcendence experience. If her transcendence experience is considered without reference to the foreground element, the aunt will be seen too much apart from the other characters like Natalie and Wilhelm, and thus her importance for each of them will be lost.

If Gundolf, despite his enthusiasm for Goethe's characters, was limited in his observation of them, he is still poles apart from Karl Schlechta, who shows hardly any sympathy for either the 'schöne Seele' or Natalie. The critics usually treat the aunt more harshly than they do Natalie; and so when we read of Natalie in Schlechta's book that 'her purity (Reinheit) and charm are inborn impotence (Unver-

---

14 Ibid., p. 516.
15 Ibid., p. 515.
16 Ibid.
17 Ibid.
18 Ibid., p. 516.

mögen)'[19] we can hardly expect that the aunt will be treated favourably.

Schlechta stresses the theme of the aunt's sickness:

> The *Confession* of Natalie's aunt begins with the birth of the 'soul' in and from a serious illness.[20]

Then he refers to the second haemorrhage and finally to the sickness and death in the family which, he says ironically, 'provide a great stimulus for her quest of self'. He concludes:

> The whole existence of this woman is sickness—sickness interrupted by short spells of diet and caution.[21]

The exaggeration of this judgment is apparent: the first haemorrhage occurred when the aunt was eight years old,[22] and the second one did not occur till she was a young woman—after the Narziss episode,[23] which must have been a good ten to fifteen years later. It is true that her constitution was frail, but we have seen from our analysis of the text that the effects of her illness were positive. Her sickness as such is not stressed. In a book about sixty pages in length, there are two brief mentions of the haemorrhages: one at the beginning, and one in the middle. This hardly justifies the judgment that her whole existence is sickness.

The link for Schlechta between her 'sickness' and her religion is direct. Physical sickness will be matched on a psychological plane by a corresponding 'sickness'. Her orientation towards her body is sick (versetzt).[24] This disorder affects her religious attitudes: Schlechta mentions[25] the adventure she had as a child with a

> charming little angel that was clothed in white, had golden wings and bestowed attention on her.

> einem reizenden kleinen Engel, der in weissem Gewand und goldnen Flügeln sich sehr um mich bemühte.[26]

This happened shortly after her illness while she was eight years old. Given a child's capacity to dream and its inability to conceive of God

19 Schlechta, *Goethes 'Wilhelm Meister'*, p. 229.
20 Ibid., p. 28.
21 Ibid.
22 *Lehrjahre*, p. 358, 5f.
23 Ibid., p. 386.
24 Schlechta, *Goethes 'Wilhelm Meister'*, p. 28.
25 Ibid., p. 28f.
26 *Lehrjahre*, p. 359, 11ff.

in terms any different from those it uses to understand its parents or friends, it would be premature to interpret this experience in terms of maladjustment. Religious 'experience' on a child's level is the smallest beginning, and it seems exaggerated to interpret its manifestations in terms of badly adjusted sexuality. Of course, Schlechta sees these erotic overtones in the light of the aunt's later erotically flavoured attitude towards the 'Invisible Friend'. In this he seems to ignore the mystical tradition in which the pietist aunt's experience is to be understood. Her identification with the piety of espousal in the Bible, in St Bernard of Clairvaux, the Spanish mystics and Count Zinzendorf's religious writings can be justified without our needing to fall back on interpretations like the one Schlechta has proposed. The tradition is so strong that we could rightly assume some form of erotic expression to be normal in a religion that stresses love. If the mystic tries to express his relationship to God, i.e., his love for God, he only has human comparisons at his disposal. No analogy is so suitable as that of the man-woman relationship to express the rapport between God and the soul: the male role is used to express the initiative, force and strength of God in his dealings with the soul of the mystic. The more typically female qualities of receptivity, passivity, openness, dedication, are suitable expression for the attitude of the soul (whether of a male or a female mystic) with regard to God. It is true that the mystics themselves regard their profound knowledge of God as basically unutterable. But in so far as they are interested in referring to it at all, one of the most favoured images they resort to is that of the soul and its spouse. Thus, given the mystical context of the book which we have dwelt on above in the introduction and conclusion, we need not, with Schlechta, be shocked to find that the 'young girl loves God and her fiancé in a strikingly similar way.'[27] In our analysis above we have shown that, despite all similarity in her relationship to God and to Narziss, her love for each of them is differentiated exactly as her involvement with the background and foreground elements is differentiated. With the aunt there is no confusion of two distinct planes of the kind we found in Novalis' poem.[28] The aunt not only distinguishes foreground and background, but is able to describe their differences and their different effects on her. Hers seems to be a much finer awareness than Schlechta suspects. The results of our analysis would seem to indicate, negatively, that the destructive criticism exercised by Schlechta is exaggerated and, positively, that there is much more depth and life in the aunt's experience than Schlechta himself was aware of.

27 Schlechta, *Goethes 'Wilhelm Meister'*, p. 28.
28 See above, p. 22f.

Other authors refer to the aunt in considerably less detail than those already discussed. They treat her with a mixture of scepticism and goodwill: scepticism, because her religiosity seems foreign to Goethe's world, and goodwill, because of the positive contribution she is evidently meant to make towards Wilhelm's inner development.

A typical example of the scepticism is found in H. A. Korff's work on *Geist der Goethezeit* (p. 335). When discussing the phenomenon 'schöne Seele', he says:

> But in this connection the *schöne Seele* is by no means the strange figure whose *Confession* we read in the sixth book, but . . . Natalie . . .

The aunt is a 'strange figure'—and a further judgment, concerning Natalie, goes hand in hand with this:

> Natalie has thereby herself become a goddess, a person *without flesh and blood*. (p. 336)

Here is another indication that an author's judgment of Natalie can be predicted from the judgment he forms of her aunt. It is to be hoped that our account of the aunt has shown that she is not a strange figure. What influence this result has on our judgment of Natalie would be the subject of a further study. In any case, as regards the aunt, it is not enough to accept Korff's judgment of her—which he does not substantiate—but we need to rely on careful reference to the text.

In his book on Goethe, Emil Staiger uses an expression, in referring to the aunt, that reminds us of Korff's judgment. He refers to the *Confession* as 'information about a strange person' (Auskunft über ein seltsames Wesen).[29] He refers to her life and circumstances as the

> peculiar conditions under which so pure and yet so confusing a manifestation of a true person as the aunt can develop.[30]

Despite the strangeness he finds in her, Staiger still finds her 'pure' (lauter) and 'true' (wahr). She is purely her own type, and—more important still—truly human. He insists on the non-Goethean elements in her makeup: her confession of sin, her tender conscience. These, as Staiger is clearly right in saying, are completely foreign to Goethe. Staiger himself would, however, admit that they can still be found in genuine people and thus do not disqualify the aunt in our eyes.

At the same time, Staiger finds in her an illustration of Goethe's

---

29 Staiger, *Goethe*, p. 141.
30 Ibid.

view, that in Christianity preoccupation with the sphere of sense can become perverted, can

> turn itself inwards and in the dim depths of the heart conjure up all the joys and pains which should be allowed to develop in the sun's light and in free contact with the natural and beautiful created world.[31]

On the basis of our findings we can seriously dispute this interpretation of the aunt. As we have seen, Goethe's picture of her is primarily positive, and he underlines this by having her reject the penitential methods of the Francke school of pietism in Halle. Even when she becomes conscious of sin, her religious experience is not essentially different from what it has been. She sees her 'Invisible Friend' now more specifically as the Christian Redeemer; but her submission to this Redeemer is just a deepening of the positive relationship she has enjoyed for years:

> When the first moment of rapture was over, I noticed that I had earlier on been familiar with this state of soul; but I had never felt it so strongly as this.

> Als das erste Entzücken vorüber war, bemerkte ich, dass mir dieser Zustand der Seele schon vorher bekannt gewesen; allein ich hatte ihn nie in dieser Stärke empfunden.[32]

We have been led to the conclusion that the aunt's attitude towards sin represents a modification of the pietist point of view.[33] Thus, rather than to stress that this image of the aunt is foreign to Goethe, it is worth noting that Goethe has presented his pietist friend in a way which is much more acceptable to him than is pietism itself.

Staiger himself admits that the

> torment of sin finally yields to an unruffled peace in God. And thus it is possible for a rounded religious experience to be united to a rounded culture like that represented by the uncle.[34]

This means that Staiger's view of the aunt is basically positive. The analysis we have presented is an attempt to highlight the experience on which such a positive view of the aunt should be based.

To sum up, our study of the transcendence experience found in the *Confession* should have served two functions in literary criticism:

---

31 Ibid., p. 141f.
32 *Lehrjahre*, p. 395, 9ff.
33 See above, p. 106.
34 Staiger, *Goethe*, p. 142.

firstly, the positive function of helping us to focus accurately on the life and sources of life as they are revealed to us in the book—thus opening up the novel in a way that helps us to appreciate its value; secondly, by having shown the life in the book, it should have performed the negative function of countering criticism based on insufficient observation.

Bibliography

PRIMARY SOURCES

Goethe. *Briefe (1764-86)*. Edited by K. R. Mandelkow. Hamburger Ausgabe, vol. 1. 1962.
—— *Wilhelm Meisters Lehrjahre*. Artemis-Verlag: Zurich 1948. Zurich: Artemis-Verlag, 1948.
—— *Wilhelm Meisters Lehrjahre*. Hamburg, 1962.
—— *Wilhelm Meister*. Translated by T. Carlyle. London and Toronto: Everyman, 1912.
—— *Wilhelm Meisters Theatralische Sendung*. Frankfurt and Hamburg 1960.
—— *Wilhelm Meisters Wanderjahre*. Hamburg, 1961.
Dollinger, H., ed. *Der Briefwechsel zwischen Schiller und Goethe*. Stuttgart, 1948.
Klettenberg, Susanna Catherina von. *Reliquien*. Hamburg, 1849.

WORKS ON THE 'SCHÖNE SEELE'

Dechent, H. *Goethes schöne Seele*. Gotha, 1896.
Funck, H., ed. *Susanna von Klettenberg, Bekenntnisse, Schriften und Briefe*. Leipzig, 1912.
Müller, H. F. 'Zur Geschichte des Begriffs "schöne Seele".' *Germ.-Rom. Monatsschrift* 7 (1914).
Schmeer, Hans. 'Der Begriff der schönen Seels besonders bei Wieland und in der deutschen Literatur des 18. Jahrhunderts.' *Germanische Studien* 44 (1926).
Schmidt, E. In *Richardson, Rousseau und Goethe*. (Appendix 4, on the 'schöne Seele'). Jena, 1875.
Waldberg, Max von. 'Der Begriff der schönen Seele'. In *Studien und Quellen zur Geschichte des Romans*. Berlin, 1910.

WORKS ON 'WILHELM MEISTER'

Angelloz, J. J. *Goethe*. Paris, 1949. (pp. 207-19).

115

Beriger, Hanno. *Goethe und der Roman. Studien zu Wilhelm Meisters Lehrjahren.* Zurich, 1955.

Blackall, E. 'Sense and Nonsense in Goethe's Wilhelm Meisters Lehrjahre'. *Deutsche Beitr. z. geistigen Überlieferung* 5 (Berne, 1965): 49-72.

—— 'Wilhelm Meister's Pious Pilgrimage'. In *German Life and Letters.* Vol. 18. Oxford, 1965. (pp. 246-52).

Borcherdt, H. H. *Der Roman der Goethezeit.* Urach and Stuttgart, 1949.

Bruford, W. H. *Goethe's Wilhelm Meister as a Picture and a Criticism of Society.* Publications of the English Goethe Society, 1933. (pp. 20-45)

Eichner, Hans. 'Zur Deutung von "Wilhelm Meisters Lehrjahren".' *Jahrb. des Fr. Dt. Hochstifts* (1966): 165-96.

Fries, Albert. *Stilistische Beobachtungen zu Wilhelm Meister.* Berlin, 1912.

Gerhard, Melitta. *Der deutsche Entwicklungsroman bis zu Goethes Wilhelm Meister.* Halle, 1926.

Gundolf, Friedrich. *Goethe.* Berlin, 1916.

Hass, Hans-Egon. 'Goethe. Wilhelm Meisters Lehrjahre'. In *Der Deutsche Roman. Vom Barock bis zur Gegenwart. Struktur und Geschichte.* Edited by Benno von Wiese. Vol. 1. Düsseldorf, 1963.

Hatfield, Henry. 'Wilhelm Meisters Lehrjahre and "Progressive Universalpoesie".' *Germanic Review* 36 (1961): 221-29.

Henkel, Arthur. 'Versuch über den "Wilhelm Meister".' *Ruperto Carola* 31 (Heidelberg, 1962): 59-67.

Hering, R. *Wilhelm Meister und Faust.* Frankfurt am Main, 1952.

Heselhaus, Clemens. 'Die Wilhelm Meister-Kritik der Romantiker und die Romantische Romantheorie'. In *Nachahmung und Illusion.* Edited by H. R. Jauss. Munich, 1964.

Jantz, Harold. 'Die Ehrfurcht in Goethe's "Wilhelm Meister". Ursprung und Bedeutung'. *Euphorion* 48 (Heidelberg, 1954): 1-18.

Jenisch, Erich. ' "Dass Klassische nenne ich das Gesunde und das Romantische das Kranke". Goethes Kritik der Romantik'. *Goethe. Neue Folge des Jhbs. der G. Gesell.* 19 (Weimar, 1957): 50-79.

Jockers, Ernst. 'Faust und Meister, zwei polare Gestalten'. In *Mit Goethe. Gesammelte Aufsätze.* Heidelberg, 1957. (pp. 148-59)

Korff, H. A. *Geist der Goethezeit.* Vol. 2. Leipzig, 1955-59.

Lange, Victòr. *Goethe's Craft of Fiction.* Publications of the English Goethe Society, no. 22, 1953. (pp. 31-63)

Lukács, Georg. 'Wilhelm Meisters Lehrjahre'. In *Goethe und seine Zeit.* Berne, 1947. (pp. 31-47)

May, Kurt. ' "Wilhelm Meisters Lehrjahre", ein Bildungsroman?' *Deutsche V. jh.schrift* 31 (1957): 1-37.

—— 'Weltbild und innere Form der Klassik und Romantik im "Wilhelm Meister" und "Heinrich von Ofterdingen".' In *Form und Bedeutung. Interpretationen deutscher Dichtung des 18. und 19. Jahrhunderts.* (Stuttgart, 1957): 161-77.

(Alexander)-Meyer, Eva. *Goethes Wilhelm Meister.* Munich, 1947.

Meyer, H. "Raumgestaltung und Raumsymbolik in der Erzählkunst'. *Studium Generale* 10/10 (1957): 620-30.

Müller, Günther. *Gestaltung-Umgestaltung in Goethes Wilhelm Meisters Lehrjahren,* Halle, 1949.

Müller, Joachim. 'Phasen der Bildungsidee im "Wilhelm Meister".' *Goethe. Neue Folge des Jhbs. der G. Gesell.* 24 (Weimar, 1962): 58-80.

Olzien, Otto Heinrich. *Der Satzbau in Wilhelm Meisters Lehrjahren.* Leipzig, 1933.

Pascal, Roy. *The German Novel: Studies.* Manchester University Press, 1956. (pp. 3-29)

Rausch, Jurgen. 'Lebensstufen in Goethes Wilhelm Meister'. *D. V. jhschr.* 20 (1942): 65-114.

Reiss, Hans. *Goethes Romane.* Berne and Munich, 1963.

Riemann, Robert. *Goethes Romantechnik,* Leipzig, 1902.

Schlechta, Karl. *Goethes 'Wilhelm Meister'.* Frankfurt am Main, 1953.

Schmitt, Paul. 'Zu "Wilhelm Meisters Lehrjahren".' In *Religion, Idee und Staat. Aus dem Nachlass.* Edited by Roques von Beit. Berne, 1959. (pp. 571-98)

Staiger, Emil. *Goethe.* Vol. 2 (1786-1814). Zurich and Freiburg im Br., 1956. (pp. 128-74)

Staroste, W. 'Zum epischen Aufbau der Realität in Goethes "Wilhelm Meister".' *Wirkendes Wort* (Düsseldorf, 1961): 34-45.

Steiner, Jacob. *Sprache und Stilwandel in Goethes 'Wilhelm Meister'.* Zurich, 1959.

Storz, Gerhard. 'Die Lieder aus Wilhelm Meister'. *Deutschunterricht* 7 (Stuttgart, 1949): 36ff. (Edited by Robert Ulshöfer.)

—— *Goethe-Vigilien.* Stuttgart, 1953.

Vietor, Karl. *Goethe.* Berne, 1949. (pp. 129-50)

Wundt, Max. *Goethes Wilhelm Meister und die Entwicklung des modernen Lebensideals.* Berlin and Leipzig, 1932. (pp. 211-39 in particular)

MORE GENERAL WORKS

Beyer, Marianne. *Empfindsamkeit, Sturm und Drang.* Leipzig, 1936.

Beyer-Fröhlich, Marianne. *Pietismus und Rationalismus*. Leipzig, 1933.

Boeschenstein, H. *Deutsche Gefühlskultur, T.I. 1770-1830*. Berne, 1954.

Bruford, W. H. *Culture and Society in Classical Weimar*. Cambridge, 1962.

Chadwick, Owen. *The Reformation*. London, 1965.

Cragg, G. R. *The Church and the Age of Reason* (1648-1789). Middlesex, 1960.

Flitner, Wilhelm. *Goethe im Spätwerk*. Hamburg, 1947. (pp. 19-56: Die religiöse Jugendentwicklung Goethes')

Garrigou-Lagrange. *Mystik und christliche Vollendung*. Augsburg, 1927.

Götting, Franz. 'Die Christusfrage in der Freundschaft zwischen Goethe und Lavater'. *Goethe. Neue Folge des Jahrbuches der Goethe-Gesellschaft* 19 (Weimar, 1957): 28-49.

Grosser, A. "Le Jeune Goethe et le piétisme'. *Etudes Germaniques* (Lyon, 1949): 203-212.

Guinaudeau, O. 'Les rapports de Goethe et de Lavater'. *Etudes Germaniques* (Lyon, 1949): 213-26.

Günther, H. R. G. *Jung-Stilling*. Munich, 1948.

—— 'Psychologie des deutschen Pietismus'. *Deutsche Vierteljahrsschrift* 4 (1926).

Hoffmeister, Johannes. *Goethe und der deutsche Idealismus*. Leipzig, 1932.

James, W. *The varieties of Religious Experience*. New York, 1961.

Jantz, Harold. 'Die Grundstruktur Goetheschen Denkens'. *Euphorion* 48 (Heidelberg, 1954): 153-70.

Kluckhohn, Paul. *Die Auffassung der Liebe in der Literatur des 18. Jahrhunderts*. Third impression. Tubingen, 1966.

—— *Das Ideengut der deutschen Romantik*. Fifth impression. Tubingen, 1966.

—— 'Goethes Bild vom Menschen'. *Studium Generale* (Berlin, 1949): 354-61.

Knappen, Marshall M. *Tudor Puritanism*. Gloucester, Mass., 1963.

Lämmerzahl, Elfride. *Der Sündenfall in der Philosophie des deutschen Idealismus*. Berlin, 1934. (pp. 97-104)

Langen, August. *Der Wortschatz des deutschen Pietismus*. Second edition. Tubingen, 1967.

—— 'Pietismus'. In *Reallexikon der deutschen Literaturgeschichte*. Vol. 3. Second impression (1966). (pp. 103-114)

Löwith, Karl. *Von Hegel zu Nietzsche*. Stuttgart, 1941. (pp. 17-43: 'Goethe und Hegel')

Mahrholz, Werner. *Der deutsche Pietismus*. Berlin, 1921.

Meinhold, P. 'Der junge Goethe und die Geschichte des Christentums'. *Saeculum* 1 (1950): 196-227.

—— 'Die Konfessionen im Urteil Goethes'. *Saeculum* 7 (1956): 79-106.

Möbus, Gerhard. *Die Christusfrage in Goethes Leben und Werk.* Osnabrück, 1964.

Namorwicz, F. *Pietismus und die deutsche Kultur des 18. Jahrhunderts.* Weimarer Beiträge, 13,3.

Obenauer, K. J. *Goethe in seinem Verhältnis zur Religion.* Jena, 1923. (pp. 15-30: 'Der junge Goethe')

Ohly, Friedrich. 'Goethes Ehrfurchten—ein ordo caritatis, I: Der ordo caritatis von Augustin bis zum 17. Jahrhundert'. *Euphorion* 55, 4, 2 (Heidelberg, 1961): 113-145.

—— 'Goethes Ehrfurchten—ein ordo caritatis, II; Goethes Landschaften der Ehrfurcht in den Wanderjahren'. *Euphorion* 55, 4, 4 (Heidelberg, 1961): 405-448.

Otto, Rudolf. *Das Gefühl des Überweltlichen (Sensus Numinosus).* Munich, 1832. (pp. 1-10)

Raabe, August. *Goethe und Luther*, Bonn, 1949.

Riemann, Carl. 'Goethes Gedanken über Kunst und Religion'. *Goethe. Neue Folge des Jahrbuches der Goethe-Gesellschaft* 24 (Weimar, 1962): 103-134.

Ritschl, A. *Geschichte des Pietismus.* Bonn, 1880. (Three volumes).

Schiller, Friedrich. *On the Aesthetic Education of Man.* Edited by E. M. Wilkinson and L. A. Willoughby. Oxford, 1967.

Schlechta, Karl. *Goethe in seinem Verhältnis zu Aristoteles.* Frankfurt am Main, 1938.

Schmidt, Martin, and Jannasch, W. *Das Zeitalter des Pietismus.* Bremen: Schünemann, 1965.

Schneider, R. 'Das ungelöste Problem. Goethes Glaube'. In *Uber Dichter und Dichtung.* Cologne, 1953. (pp. 227-46)

Schubert, Hans von. *Goethes religiöse Jugendentwicklung.* Leipzig, 1925.

Schultz, Franz. *Klassik und Romantik der Deutschen.* Second impression. Vol. 2. Stuttgart, 1952. (pp. 274-93)

Sperber, Hans. 'Der Einfluss des Pietismus auf die Sprache des 18. Jahrhunderts'. *Dt. Vierteljahrsschrift* (1930): 497-515.

Stemme, F. 'Die Säkularisation des Pietismus zur Erfahrungsseelenkunde'. *Zeitschrift für dt. Philologie* (1953).

Strich, Fritz. *Deutsche Klassik und Romantik.* Fourth impression. Berne, 1949.

Unger, Rudolf. *Hamann und die Aufklärung.* Second impression. Halle, 1925.

Waldberg, Max von. *Der empfindsame Roman in Frankreich. Erster*

Teil. Die Anfänge bis zum Beginne des 18. Jahrhunderts. Strasbourg and Berlin: Trübner, 1906.

Wieser, Max. *Der sentimentale Mensch.* Stuttgart, 1924.

Wilkinson, E. M. 'The Theological Basis of Faust's Credo'. *German Life and Letters* 10 (1957): 229-39.

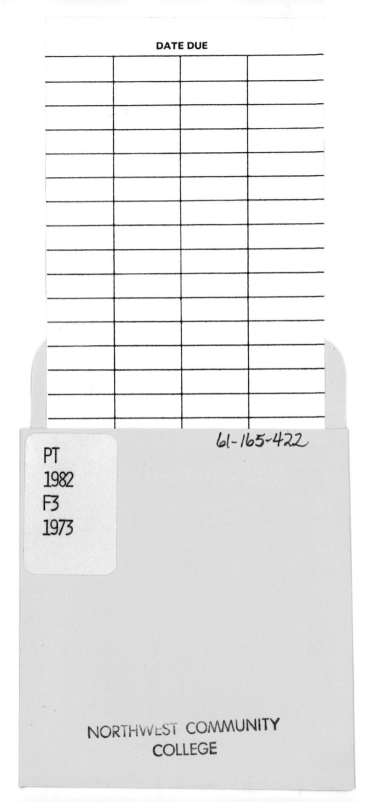